King Estate Winery
King Estate Pinot Noir Cookbook

Compiled and edited by
Stephanie Pearl Kimmel.
Photography by John Rizzo.

Includes index.

Library of Congress
Catalog Card Number
95-80582

ISBN 0-9645500-2-4

10 9 8 7 6 5 4 3 2 1

Printed in Hong Kong

PINOT NOIR COOKBOOK

TABLE OF CONTENTS

KING ESTATE
PINOT NOIR COOKBOOK

ROBERT DEL GRANDE/CAFÉ ANNIE   42
~Cinnamon Roasted Chicken with Pozole and Pears

KASPAR DONIER/KASPAR'S   46
~Goat Cheese Wrapped in Grape Leaves with Wine Braised Garlic

TODD ENGLISH/OLIVES   50
~Stracotto of Salmon Braised in Red Wine

DEAN FEARING/THE MANSION ON TURTLE CREEK   54
~Molasses Duck with Smoked Vegetable Dressing and Peach Chutney
~Rack of Lamb on Pear Purée
with Blue Cheese Bread Pudding and Port Wine Sauce

JOYCE GOLDSTEIN/SQUARE ONE   60
~Grilled Chicken in a Pomegranate Marinade
~Moroccan-Style Roast Fish with Caramelized Onions and Raisins

JEAN JOHO/EVEREST   64
~Cured Duck Salad with Mixed Baby Greens and Walnut Vinaigrette

EMERIL LAGASSE/EMERIL'S   68
~Pinot Noir Zabaglione with Red Grapes and Blue Cheese

*O*ur Pinot Noir cookbook is the
second in a series about the harmonious relationship
between food and wine. The first book, which
celebrated Pinot Gris, was so enthusiastically
received that we were encouraged to continue.
Thus, this lovely book, filled with the delicious
recipes of a select group of supremely talented chefs.

Pinot Noir's mystique is like no other. Captivating
novice and seasoned winemaker alike, the pursuit
of the great, the transcendent, Pinot Noir
experience can become a lifelong preoccupation.
The quest is compelling and the reward is wine of
legendary elegance.

Finally, I cannot introduce this book to you without
thinking of our dear and wonderful friend André
Tchelistcheff, whose passion for making Pinot Noir
will always be an inspiration. Humbly, we dedicate
this book to his memory.

KING ESTATE

At King Estate, our devotion to scaling the highest peaks of quality is as evident in our culinary program as it is in our winemaking. Our mission—to produce varietal wines (Pinot Noir, Pinot Gris and Chardonnay) of consistently exceptional quality to enhance the dining experience of all who partake of them—reflects our belief that there is a synergistic relationship between wine and food. The greatness of each is elevated by the other. We feel that understanding this connection helps us to become better winemakers. For this reason we have dedicated a significant portion of our energies and resources to the pursuit of culinary excellence.

In addition to planting hundreds of acres of meticulously tended vineyards, we have established a large, lovingly maintained organic garden and several acres of organic orchard. During our long growing season, virtually all of the produce used in King Estate's Culinary Program is grown on the Estate. We at King Estate have committed ourselves to responsible stewardship of the magnificent land we tend. In our vineyards, garden and orchards, and even in our landscaping, we have prohibited the use of chemical fertilizers, pesticides and herbicides. We have established a massive composting program, and we are continuously researching ways to improve our agriculture using organic techniques. We sincerely believe that by working in harmony with nature we will not only protect our environment but also improve the quality of our wines.

King Estate is far more than just a vineyard and winery. It is a place where many dedicated, hardworking, talented individuals work with great pride and determination to achieve a common goal: to make King Estate an enduring standard of excellence in winemaking, viticulture, agriculture and the culinary arts.

Michael Lambert
Vice President/General Manager

PINOT NOIR

*P*inot Noir, head of the noble Pinot family named for the pine cone shape of its grape clusters, boasts a venerable lineage. The Roman historian Pliny noted that Pinot Noir was being cultivated in the Burgundy region of France when the Romans invaded Gaul in the first century A.D. This vine, called *Vitis allobrogica*, had been bred from wild indigenous vines. The nobles of the Gallic tribes drank wine made from the fruit and, precociously, stored it in wooden casks instead of the clay amphorae typical of the Romans. Three hundred years later, when the Emperor Constantine visited the Côte d'Or near Beaune, he was impressed by the wine he found there.

For centuries after the Barbarian invaders drove the Romans out of Burgundy, viticultural traditions were handed down by the peasant vignerons who worked the vineyards for the wealthy landowners. But the primary credit for the survival of Pinot Noir in Burgundy must go to the monks of the Catholic Church, who enhanced the reputation of wine by using it in their sacraments and approving it as a comfort and luxury in the temporal world. These men, who had the security, resources and land to develop their vineyards, continually improved the Pinot Noir varietal through their patient experimentation and meticulous stewardship.

By the 6th century, the aristocracy of Burgundy had begun giving vineyard land to the Church at Aloxe, Beaune, Gevrey and Vosne. Between the 8th and 11th centuries, Fixin, Chassagne, Santenay, Meursault and Pommard all likewise became Church property. In 1275 the Benedictine order owned all of the vineyards around Romanée-Conti, La Romanée, La Tâche, Richebourg and Romanée-St.-Vivant, and by 1336 the Cistercians had amassed the largest single vineyard in Burgundy, Clos de Vougeot. Their abbot, upon sending several barrels of wine to the Pope, was rewarded with a cardinal's hat.

Not only those in religious orders recognized the value of Burgundy's wine. As early as the year 800, when Charlemagne acquired vineyards in Corton, he decreed that the peasants could no longer tread the grapes with their feet. This was a polite gesture, but unnecessary—the alcohol formed in fermentation is a natural antiseptic against bacteria. In the 13th century when Philip the Bold ruled the Duchy of Burgundy, he forbade the storage in his realm of any wine other than "burgundy" and, foreshadowing today's strict controls, banned the blending of Gamay with Pinot Noir.

When Philip the Bold inherited Flanders through a propitious marriage, he introduced Pinot Noir to the court in Brussels. This was a rare excursion, for Burgundy's landlocked position had made distribution difficult. Because the winegrowing regions of Bordeaux and Spain were situated near sea ports, clarets and sherries had begun to enjoy an international reputation, but the wines of Burgundy were still mainly appreciated closer to home. Not until the 16th century, when the Burgundian Parliament developed a new tax system to finance the construction of canals linking the Saône river with the Seine and the Loire, did the wines of Burgundy become known to connoisseurs outside the region. Finally, in the 19th century, with the advent of railways that quickly carried wine overland to ports, Pinot Noir became a wine for the world.

In 1789, the French Revolution drastically changed the winemaking industry in Burgundy. The vineyards were seized from the nobles and the Church, and a comprehensive redistribution of the land led to extensive subdivision and fragmentation. French inheritance laws exacerbated the situation—with real property shared equally by surviving family members, the formerly vast holdings soon became tiny plots tended by individual grape growers. From these circumstances evolved the typically Burgundian system, still in place today, in which the négociants blend wines from small lots to a desired style, while also managing the cellaring, shipping and distribution.

France continues to maintain the world's largest planting of Pinot Noir, mostly on the Côte d'Or but also in Champagne where its presence in the blends provides sparkling wines with structure and longevity. Pinot Noir in Alsace is used to make a light aromatic red wine, and in Sancerre, the Savoie and the Jura it yields small quantities of pale red wines.

In Germany, where Pinot Noir is called Spätburgunder, 10,000 acres are planted, primarily in the South.

The wine is very much loved in Germany itself but is not generally exported because the style is not typical—due to the difficulty of fully ripening grapes in that climate, the wine is pale and more than a little sweet. Italy produces modest examples of Pinot Noir (Pinot Nero), the exception being those grown on the upper slopes of the Alto Adige valley in the North, where the temperatures at that altitude prolong the growing season sufficiently to permit a more complex wine. In the Valais district of Switzerland, Pinot Noir is blended into the well-known Dôle wines, and Oeil de Perdrix, which is vinified white, is a slightly bubbly version. Pinot Noir is also planted across Eastern Europe—in Austria, Czechoslavakia, Hungary, Bulgaria, Serbia, Macedonia—and even farther east, in China. And in certain microclimates of Australia, New Zealand, South Africa and Chile winemakers have had some notable successes with Pinot Noir.

In the United States, Pinot Noir is primarily planted on the West Coast, in California and Oregon. Growers in California's Napa Valley began planting Pinot Noir in the thirties (Louis Martini even had the vision to plant it in Carneros, a barren, fog-shrouded stretch along San Pablo Bay just south of Napa, that was considered agriculturally worthless at the time). The Napa acreage in Pinot Noir continued to grow steadily until the early eighties with a large part of the crop going into méthode champenoise sparkling wines. At that time those winemakers in Napa who had been struggling to make consistently good Pinot Noir tended to switch to other varietals or to look elsewhere for more suitable growing areas. With a nod to Mr. Martini, winegrowers have found the cool and windy Carneros region to be a better spot for Pinot Noir. Plantings of Pinot Noir are on the increase there as well as in other parts of California with microclimates that mitigate the hot summers. The Russian River area of Sonoma County and the Anderson Valley near Mendocino have produced some outstanding Pinot as have the Central Coast appellations of Santa Maria, Santa Barbara, Santa Ynez and Mt. Harlan. California Pinot Noir typically gets its deep color and high tannin from prolonged maceration after harvest. The result is ripe and rich, usually opaque and plummy, in a style reminiscent of the big California Cabernets. Recently a movement toward aging the wine for less time in oak barrels has elicited praise from many critics.

Pinot Noir was introduced into Oregon in the late sixties. Oregon wine pioneer David Lett, while studying viticulture at the University of California at Davis, decided to follow his heart and specialize in growing Pinot Noir. His opinion, based on his research, was that growing Pinot in California would always be problematic, so he set out to Burgundy to see first-hand the conditions under which it thrives. When he returned to the United States he moved to the Willamette Valley, convinced that it was the ideal situtation for growing cool climate varietals. He planted his Eyrie vineyards and was soon joined by fellow visionaries Dick Erath and Dick Ponzi. When the vines matured and they tasted those first lovely wines, they knew they had been right.

Pinot Noir is now the most widely planted grape variety in Oregon, the long cool growing season suiting it perfectly. Crush in Oregon often comes as much as six weeks later than harvest in California. This extra time on the vine allows the levels of acids, tannins and anthocyanins (compounds that give color) to develop more fully, adding complexity and structure, as well as flavor to the wines. Oregon Pinot Noirs are generally more Burgundian: translucent with bright berry fruit, feminine and silky, with understated oak. Each summer Oregon hosts the International Pinot Noir Celebration, an intense and extraordinary three days of seminars and tastings

with hundreds of representatives from all of the major Pinot growing regions of the world.

At King Estate we have made a monumental commitment to Pinot Noir, both in our viticulture and in our production. To enable us to make Pinot Noir with exceptional complexity, we have planted one of the most, if not *the* most, clonally diverse

vineyards in North America. We have 16 different clones of Pinot Noir planted on the Estate's property. In addition, we have established long term contracts with more than 30 of the most distinguished Pinot Noir vineyards in Oregon. The subtle nuances of character in grapes from different clones and from various parts of the state offer us a broad palate of aromas, textures and flavors from which to blend Pinot Noir of outstanding complexity and consistent quality.

At our winery each individual lot of grapes is handled separately, allowing our talented winemaking team to extract the finest characteristics from the delicate Pinot Noir grapes. To accomplish this feat, the winery is equipped with 51 small fermentation tanks specifically designed to ensure the gentle extraction of aroma and flavor components from the grapes, preserving their fragile intensity. This tender, hands-on treatment of each small lot is essential to the production of the finest Pinot Noir. After fermentation, each lot is aged separately in French oak barrels. At the end of aging, before the blending process begins, each lot is evaluated and those not meeting our rigorous standards are set aside to be sold off in bulk. Blending the Pinot Noir from the remaining lots is a slow and painstaking process, but

the result is representative of the finest the vintage has to offer. The King Estate Pinot Noir is then aged in the bottle to further soften and refine the aroma, flavor and texture of the wine. When the wine is released, it is ready to be enjoyed, perhaps with one of the fabulous recipes that follow.

PAIRING PINOT NOIR AND FOOD

Matching wine and food is a matter of personal perception, but there are some general principles that can serve as guidelines. Foods are made up of flavor components: sweetness, bitterness, acid, salt and fat. In wine, the components are fruit, sugar, tannin, acid and alcohol. The most successful pairings are created by either contrasting the elements or emphasizing their similarity—in complex dishes you may be doing some of each. The important thing is to learn to recognize these building blocks of flavor and experiment with different combinations that appeal to your own palate.

Pinot Noir, with its lovely fruit and touch of peppery spice, its smoky, earthy undertones of mushrooms and truffles, is a perfect complement to a variety of foods. It is a natural partner to roasted and grilled beef, lamb, pork and game, as the brightness of the fruit and well-balanced acid temper the fattiness of the meats. That Burgundian classic, boeuf à la bourguignonne—rich beef, smoky bacon, earthy mushrooms, sweet onions, fruity wine with just the right amount of acid—shows a harmony of flavors within the dish itself as well as with the wine of the region. At King Estate we have had great success serving a simple beef tenderloin with morel sauce, rack of lamb with mint béarnaise, and pork tenderloin with tapenade.

The richness of duck invites accompaniment with elements of fruit and acidity—a perfect example is the classic duck à l'orange. Because richness, fruit and acidity are reflected in a well-balanced Pinot Noir, we have enjoyed the combination of duck breast with a Pinot Noir sauce accented with tayberry vinegar and juniper berries, served with a fig compote. A glass of Pinot Noir also enhances duck confit with grilled pears and wilted greens; and roast duck with orange and olive sauce—contemporary pairings that carry on a culinary tradition.

Venison is a favorite at King Estate in the fall: medallions seared as one would a pepper steak, accompanied by a chanterelle and potato galette— or a venison sausage with pear and huckleberry chutney. Rabbit grilled with mustard and rosemary or braised in a civet rich with Pinot Noir and herbs is also delightful.

In Oregon, Pinot Noir is often served with native salmon, either grilled or roasted. This pairing works especially well with a red wine or meat stock based sauce, but it is also sublime with no sauce at all. Trout broiled with sage and bacon, thyme-crusted red snapper with roasted garlic mashed potatoes, and grilled ahi tuna on white bean purée are excellent examples of how well seafood goes with Pinot Noir.

The talented chefs you will meet on the following pages have created dishes that are outstanding with Pinot Noir. Some recipes are complex, some simple; some celebrate the ingredients of a particular region, some are more classical. All are delicious. So enjoy reading about the chefs, get in a good stock of Pinot Noir, and have fun with the recipes—a taste of America's most spectacular restaurants in the comfort of home.

King Estate

PINOT NOIR COOKBOOK

MARK BAKER

FOUR SEASONS HOTEL
CHICAGO

*M*ark Baker, executive chef of the Four Seasons Hotel in Chicago, hails from New England. His interest in cooking began at home, where he prepared meals alongside his mother who encouraged him, and watched Julia Child who tutored him from the television screen. After a course at a regional vocational school, he apprenticed at the Greenbrier Resort in White Sulphur Springs, West Virginia. His experience there solidified his belief that "being a chef is the greatest job on earth."

After Greenbrier, Mark joined the Four Seasons Hotel in Washington D.C., where he worked his way up the ranks under Doug McNeill. Five years later, in 1985, he became the executive chef at the Four Seasons Hotel in Vancouver, British Columbia, at 25 the youngest executive chef in the history of the Four Seasons group. In 1987, he returned to his home town of Boston to become executive chef of the Four Seasons Hotel there. In 1991, his culinary journey brought him to his current position in Chicago.

At Seasons, the showcase restaurant of this Five-Star, Five-Diamond property, Mark leads a staff of 50, creating inspired seasonal dishes made from unique American regional ingredients. In his research for Seasons, he worked with the Department of Agriculture tracking down the best small growers and suppliers in the country. He continues to meet with them on a regular basis to control how food is grown and delivered to the restaurant. His talent and dedication have been rewarded with excellent reviews in *Esquire, Harper's Bazaar, GQ, Food and Wine, The New York Times* and *Condé Nast Traveler.*

Another of Mark's passions is wine, and as director of the Four Seasons wine program he has focused on pairing the fine wines of premium American producers with his cuisine. The notes he sent along with his recipe illustrate his knowledge and enthusiasm: "…Burgundian reserve…a sense of earthiness and wild mushrooms. As the wine opened, it revealed wonderful nuances of smokiness and cherry, along with a firm backbone. To partner this wonderful wine, I chose the smokiness of bacon, the richness and velvet texture of yellowfin tuna, and the slight sweetness of corn and lobster."

Peppercorn Crusted Ahi Tuna
with Lobster Mashed Potatoes
and Illinois Corn Sauce

Serves 4

This recipe may look complex and lengthy, but it actually involves just a few simple steps that can be done ahead and brought together at the last minute. This would be an impressive main course for a small dinner party.

Ingredients

4 6-ounce, super fresh ahi tuna steaks, cut from the
  loin and at least 1/2 inch thick
1 teaspoon pink peppercorns, lightly crushed
1 teaspoon black peppercorns, lightly crushed
Coarse salt

Corn Sauce

2 ounces unsalted butter
2 to 3 ears fresh corn to yield 2 cups kernels
1 large shallot, finely minced
3/4 cup dry white wine
6 ounces cold unsalted butter cut into 1/2-inch cubes
1 tablespoon chopped chives

Lobster Mashed Potatoes

1 pound Yukon Gold potatoes, or substitute other
  floury potatoes such as russets
4 tablespoons coarse salt
4 ounces cold unsalted butter, cut into 1/2-inch cubes

4 slices smoked bacon, cut into julienne strips
  and cooked crispy
2 tablespoons crème fraîche, or you may
  substitute sour cream
2 scallions, sliced on the bias into thin ovals
Salt and pepper to taste
6 ounces cooked lobster meat, cut into
  1/4-inch cubes

Chive Oil

1 bunch chives, or if from the garden, a nice handful
1 cup good quality olive oil

Lightly coat ahi tuna steaks with a mix of the peppercorns, then season lightly with coarse salt.

To prepare corn sauce, shuck corn and remove silk. Rinse well and remove kernels from cob with a sharp knife. In a medium saucepan, melt 2 ounces butter. Add the corn kernels and sweat them over low heat for about 3 minutes, stirring occasionally, then add the shallots and white wine. Simmer gently for about 10 minutes. Remove from heat, pour contents into blender and slowly blend to emulsify. When the sauce begins to come together, start adding the 6 ounces of cubed butter one cube at a time. Continue until all the butter has been incorporated into the sauce. Strain the sauce through a coarse sieve or chinois and hold over very low heat until ready to serve.

To prepare lobster mashed potatoes, wash potatoes well, but do not peel. In a large saucepan, cover the potatoes with water equal to double the volume of the potatoes. Add 4 tablespoons of coarse salt. Boil potatoes over medium high heat until knife tender, but not mushy—about 25 minutes. Drain and allow to cool slightly. Using a kitchen towel to protect your hands, peel the potatoes and pass them through a ricer or food mill. Put the potatoes back into the saucepan over low heat and gently fold in the 4 ounces of cubed butter, one cube at a time. Add the crème fraîche, cooked bacon and green onions. Season to taste. Hold over warm water. (The cooked lobster is added just before serving.)

To make chive oil, place chives in blender and add the olive oil. Place blender on high speed and purée until the oil turns a brilliant green, about 5 minutes. Strain and decant into a squeeze bottle or a bottle with a pour spout. (This will keep 2 to 3 weeks in the refrigerator and makes a lovely embellishment for many dishes.)

Heat a teflon-coated skillet to medium high and brush the bottom with olive oil. Add steaks and sear for 2 minutes on each side for medium rare tuna. Transfer to a clean towel, wrap and keep warm.

To assemble dish, warm corn sauce to just below simmer and stir in the chives. Warm potatoes until steaming and fold in lobster pieces. Allow to cook for another minute or so to warm lobster.

In the center of a large dinner plate, spoon a quarter of the mashed potatoes into a neat mound (use a ring mold if you have one). Slice tuna in half on the bias and arrange on top of potatoes. Spoon corn sauce around the tuna. Decorate the blank space with a few dots of chive oil.

ALISON BARSHAK

STRIPED BASS
PHILADELPHIA

Bitten by the cooking bug at an early age, Alison Barshak wanted to attend culinary school; her parents, however, insisted that she get a college education. She solved the problem by majoring in fun at college while working in restaurants. Now, although she is only 33 years old, she finds herself at the helm of Philadelphia's most popular kitchen, having worked her way from prep cook to top chef positions at some of the city's best eateries. Alison's extensive travels in Europe, South America, Mexico and the U.S. have profoundly influenced her eclectic cuisine. She brings an extraordinary array of ingredients to Striped Bass' all-seafood menu.

Striped Bass occupies—with great style—the offices of a former brokerage house on Walnut Street. Its marble pillars, 28-foot ceilings, towering palm trees and luxurious banquettes combine to evoke the atmosphere of an exotic grand hotel. Along a back wall is the full exhibition kitchen; a spectacular 16-foot sculpture of a leaping bass disguises the hood and duct work. On this dramatic stage, Alison directs her legion of sous chefs, personally inspecting every dish. At her highly sought-after Chef's Table, guests sit right in the hubbub of the kitchen to enjoy a multi-course meal planned and prepared by Alison.

The restaurant, which opened in 1994, was named "Best New Restaurant of the Year" by *Esquire* and one of the "Hot New Restaurants" by *Bon Appétit. Town and Country* named Striped Bass the "hottest place in Philadelphia." Alison has been honored as one of America's Rising Star Chefs and has appeared in the prestigious PBS series of the same name.

Cedar Planked Sea Bass
with Baby Turnips and Beets
and Dried Cherry-Rhubarb Compote

Serves 4

Cooking on wooden planks is a time-honored Native American method of cooking that imparts a subtle woodsy flavor. Cedar planks are available at specialty cookware shops. At the restaurant Alison prepares this dish with whole sea bass.

Ingredients

4 6- to 7-ounce filets of sea bass or other firm fish
Vegetable oil to coat

Dried Cherry-Rhubarb Compote

2 cups rhubarb, about 2 large stalks, cut in large dice
1 cup dried cherries
1/4 cup grenadine syrup
1/2 cup water
Juice of 1/2 lemon, strained
5 tablespoons sugar

1/2 pound baby chiogga beets, or
    substitute baby red beets
1/2 pound baby golden beets
1/2 pound baby turnips
Vegetable oil to coat

Salt and freshly ground pepper
1/2 pound fresh Rainier cherries, pitted, or
    substitute another dark red cherry, such as
    Bing or Republic

Soak the cedar plank in water for about 45 minutes while you proceed with the recipe. The soaking will prevent the plank from getting scorched in the hot oven.

Lightly oil the filets and season with salt and freshly ground pepper.

To prepare dried cherry-rhubarb compote, combine the rhubarb, dried cherries, grenadine, water, lemon juice and sugar in a medium saucepan. Cook over medium heat until rhubarb is soft and cherries are plump. Taste for sweetness and add more sugar if needed. Set aside until just before serving.

Wash the beets and turnips well. Set out 3 squares of aluminum foil on work surface. Put the beets on one square, the golden beets on another, and the turnips on the last. Drizzle each with vegetable oil, season with salt and freshly ground pepper and toss lightly to coat. Close up each square of foil to make a little package and place side by side on a baking sheet. Roast in a 350-degree oven until tender, about 30 minutes. Remove from oven and open packets. Allow vegetables to cool enough to handle, then slip off peels, trim ends and cut in half. Keep the vegetables warm while cooking fish.

Turn the oven up to 500 degrees. Place the cedar plank in the oven. Place the filets on the cedar plank and roast until done, 10 to 12 minutes, depending on the density of the fish.

Meanwhile, warm up the cherries and reheat the compote and the vegetables if necessary.

To assemble dish, place each filet in the center of a large dinner plate. Place vegetables and cherries decoratively around the filet, then sauce the fish liberally with the compote.

PHILIPPE BOULOT

HEATHMAN HOTEL
PORTLAND, OREGON

While still a boy in Normandy, Philippe Boulot was appointed family cook by his working parents. His mother, a hairdresser, would treat her clients to tastes of his dishes, and he was delighted by their extravagant praise. The summers of his high school years were spent on his grandmother's farm helping her prepare meals for the farm workers. They made their own cream, butter and cheese, butchered their own pork and lamb, and made all types of pâtés and sausages. This simple, but intensely flavorful farm cooking had a strong influence on the way Philippe approaches his work today. The satisfaction and encouragement of these childhood experiences led him to hotel school in Paris to further his education.

After graduation Philippe went to work for Joël Robuchon at both Hotel Nikko and Jamin, where he learned to appreciate discipline, precision and extraordinary standards of quality. His next position was at L'Archestrate with Alain Senderens, who stressed the importance of original dishes and creative presentation. This balanced training in the best kitchens of Paris led him, at age 27, to his first position as chef de cuisine at the Inn on the Park in London. There he polished his English as well as his managerial skills and began to fashion a plan to live and work in the United States with his American wife, Susan, a pastry chef, and their infant son. In San Francisco, at the Clift Hotel, he learned to adapt to American attitudes about business and life. In the summer of 1989, Philippe moved to New York for a stint at the Mark Hotel, earning it the national Best Restaurant of the Year title from *Esquire* magazine in 1992 and a Best of the Best from the Five Star-Five Diamond Awards, as well as a coveted *Meilleur Oeuvrier de France* designation from his native country. Then it was on to Portland, his wife's hometown, and the position of executive chef at the Heathman Hotel.

The Heathman is one of Portland's finest hotels, with an emphasis on superb quality and service. Philippe has wowed not only the guests but also the press. In his first year there, the restaurant was named Restaurant of the Year by *The Oregonian*. His success is due to his impeccable training and the enthusiasm with which he has embraced Oregon ingredients and the Northwest lifestyle.

Roast Fallow Venison Wrapped in Applewood Smoked Bacon with Huckleberry Grand Veneur Sauce

Serves 4

Philippe's recipe is a spectacular symphony of autumn flavors. While some of the ingredients may be difficult to locate in certain geographic areas, the result is worth the effort. For the imaginative cook, possible variations abound: instead of venison, use other game or pork; rather than huckleberries, try cranberries or currants; to replace the pom poms, substitute other wild mushrooms or very large cultivated mushrooms.

Ingredients

Huckleberry Grand Veneur Sauce

8 ounces shallots, chopped

2 ounces unsalted butter, plus 2 more ounces
    unsalted butter

6 tablespoons huckleberry jam

3 ounces fresh or frozen huckleberries, stemmed

1 bottle Pinot Noir or other dry red wine

1 cup veal demi-glace or strong veal stock

Venison Roast

28 ounces venison loin, about 2 to 3 inches in
    diameter, trimmed of silver skin

12 ounces applewood smoked bacon, thinly sliced

8 ounces caul fat, soaked in water (caul fat is
    available at specialty butcher shops)

Acorn Squash Accompaniment

2 acorn squash

4 ounces unsalted butter

4 ounces brown sugar

4 ounces bourbon

Salt and freshly ground pepper

Pom Pom Mushroom Accompaniment

1 pound pom pom mushrooms (hericium)

2 ounces olive oil

Salt and freshly ground pepper

Sage Leaf Garnish

1/4 cup olive oil

1/4 cup vegetable oil

12 large sage leaves

In a medium stainless steel or enamel saucepan, sweat the shallots with 2 ounces of the butter. Add the huckleberry jam and cook for a few minutes to slightly caramelize the sugar in the jam. Deglaze with the wine and reduce over medium high heat until the sauce is syrupy, about half an hour. Add the huckleberries and the stock and reduce to desired consistency. Whisk in the other 2 ounces of butter and season to taste with salt and pepper. The sauce can be held in a warm spot until ready to serve, then slowly reheated. It can also be made ahead up to the point before the final butter is added then refrigerated. Just before serving time, the sauce can be reheated and the butter whisked in.

Preheat the oven to 375 degrees. Wrap the venison loins with the sliced bacon, slightly overlapping slices as you wind around the loin. The ends of the loins do not need to be encased. Wring the water out of a piece of caul fat, lay it on the work surface, and place the bacon-wrapped loin on top. Completely enclose the loin in the caul fat, tucking any loose ends underneath (trim if necessary). Then place in roasting pan. Repeat with remaining loins. Roast to an internal temperature of 125 degrees for medium rare, about 15 minutes. Remove meat from oven, cover loosely with aluminum foil and let meat rest for 5 minutes before slicing.

Cut each acorn squash in half lengthwise; scoop out seeds and stringy fiber. Cut each squash half into

wedges about 1-1/2 inches thick. Trim peel from the edges. In a medium saucepan, melt the butter, add the brown sugar and bourbon and bring to a boil. Add the slices of squash and cook until soft, about 15 minutes.

While the venison is roasting and the squash cooking, cut the mushrooms in half and toss in a large bowl with the olive oil and salt and pepper. Grill them on a hot griddle, turning once, until soft and golden.

To fry the sage leaves, heat the oil in a small sauté pan, add the sage leaves and fry until crisp, 3 to 4 minutes. Drain on paper towels.

To assemble dish, slice the venison into medallions 1 inch thick and place them around the center of a large dinner plate, alternating with slices of squash and pieces of mushroom. Top each medallion with the huckleberry sauce and garnish with deep-fried sage leaves.

DANIEL BOULUD

RESTAURANT DANIEL
NEW YORK CITY

*D*aniel Boulud grew up on his family's farm just outside Lyons, France. He assisted his grandmother in the kitchen, using local, seasonal ingredients and learning the profoundly traditional cooking for which this area is celebrated. At 14 he began his professional education, perfecting his technique at a conservative two-star restaurant in Lyons. In 1972, he was named Best Apprentice of France, then went on to cook for two years with the legendary Georges Blanc at La Mère Blanc in Vonnas. The next four years were spent alongside Roger Vergé at Le Moulin de Mougins and Michel Guérard at Eugénie-les-Bains, learning the lighter, more contemporary style of cooking and artistic presentation that came to be known as Nouvelle Cuisine.

Daniel came to the United States in 1980 as chef to the European Economic Commission in Washington, D.C. He was chef at New York's Westbury and Plaza-Athénée hotels before assuming the executive chef position at Le Cirque. Within a year it had been awarded four stars in *The New York Times*. Six years later, in May 1993 when he opened his own restaurant, recognition was immediate. In 1993, Restaurant Daniel was voted Best New Restaurant by *Esquire* and the Number One Restaurant in the United States by *The International Herald Tribune*. The following year brought acclaim as Best Restaurant of the Year by *Bon Appétit*. Daniel was named Outstanding Chef in America by The James Beard Foundation, and the restaurant was awarded four stars by *The New York Times*. In 1995, Restaurant Daniel received a four-star rating from the *Mobil Travel Guide* and Daniel was inducted into The James Beard Foundation's Who's Who of Food and Beverage. In addition to his duties in the kitchen, Daniel writes the monthly column "Daniel's Dish" for *Elle Decor* and is co-owner of Feast & Fêtes, a New York catering firm.

CRISP PAUPIETTE OF SEA BASS
IN PINOT NOIR SAUCE

Serves 4

Daniel was inspired by Paul Bocuse's Rouget en Écailles de Pomme de Terre to create this version of fish filets wrapped in a crispy crust of sliced potatoes. Instead of the tiny red mullets of the original recipe, Daniel suggests sea bass. This dish can be assembled up to an hour ahead and refrigerated until it is time to sauté the fish.

INGREDIENTS

PAUPIETTE OF SEA BASS

4 7-ounce sea bass filets, skinless, with bones set
    aside for the sauce
Salt and freshly ground black pepper
1 teaspoon fresh thyme leaves, chopped
2 very large, very long baking potatoes, peeled
2 tablespoons unsalted butter, melted
1 tablespoon unsalted butter for sautéing
    the paupiettes

SAUCE

1 tablespoon vegetable oil
1/2 cup shallots, peeled and chopped
1/2 cup button mushrooms, caps only, sliced
Small sprig fresh thyme
1 cup rich chicken stock
1 bottle Pinot Noir or other dry red wine

1 tablespoon heavy cream
4 ounces unsalted butter, cut into small pieces
Pinch of sugar
Salt and freshly ground black pepper

LEEK ACCOMPANIMENT

1 tablespoon unsalted butter
2 leeks, white part only, thinly sliced
Salt and freshly ground black pepper

4 small sprigs of fresh thyme
1 tablespoon chives, minced

To prepare the paupiettes, make each filet as rectangular as possible (about 5 inches by 2 inches) by trimming off any uneven edges with a sharp knife. Salt and pepper the filets and sprinkle them with the chopped thyme. Set aside. Using a long, sharp knife, square off each side of the potatoes. Do not cut off the tips of the potatoes because you want as much length as possible—just trim off the peel. Using a mandoline or vegetable slicer, cut each potato lengthwise into extremely thin, long slices. It is critical that the potato slices be translucent and flexible so that they will easily bend around the fish. Each potato should yield about 16 slices roughly

1 inch wide (8 slices are needed to wrap one filet). Do not rinse the potato slices because leaving the starch will help them stick together. Toss the potato slices with the melted butter and a pinch of salt.

Cut a 10-inch-square piece of parchment paper and place it on the work surface. Choose 8 potato slices of approximately the same length. Place one of the sea bass filets horizontally at the top of the parchment paper so you can match the size of the potato wrap to the length of the fish. Just below the fish, lay out a slice of potato perpendicular to the fish, starting on the left. Place a second slice overlapping the first one, about 3/8 inch from the left edge. Continue overlapping the potato slices until you have covered an area equal to the length of the filet. Pick up the fish and center it horizontally in the middle of the potato slices. Fold the slices up and around the filet to completely enclose it. With the help of the parchment paper, turn the fish filet seam side down and refrigerate for half an hour to set the potato wrap. This may sound complex, but just visualize a rectangle of overlapping potato slices

large enough to wrap the fish. Once you have laid the slices out on the parchment it will be apparent how to proceed.

To prepare the sauce, heat the oil in a large pot over high heat. Add the reserved fish bones, the shallots, mushrooms and thyme sprig and cook for 8 to 10 minutes, stirring often. Add the chicken stock, bring to a boil, and cook until reduced to a glaze. Add the red wine and bring to a boil, then allow the liquid to reduce to half its volume. Using a mesh skimmer, remove and discard the fish bones. Reduce the sauce to 2 tablespoons. Add the heavy cream, stir and bring to a boil. Remove from the heat and whisk in the butter and the sugar, then salt and pepper to taste. Strain the sauce through a fine mesh strainer and keep warm on the side. If the sauce is too thick, add a little water to thin it.

To prepare the leeks, melt 1 tablespoon of butter in a pan over low heat. Add the leeks and cook until soft, about 4 minutes. Salt and pepper to taste. Keep warm on the side.

Preheat the oven to 425 degrees. Melt the remaining tablespoon of butter in a large nonstick pan over medium-high heat. Add the paupiettes and sauté until the potatoes are golden brown and crisp, about 4 or 5 minutes on each side. Do not crowd the paupiettes—use two pans if necessary—because they can be a bit tricky to turn. If the fish is very thick, finish cooking in the oven for 4 or 5 minutes more rather than letting the paupiette get overly brown in the sauté pan.

To assemble dish, place a spoonful of leeks in the middle of a large, warm dinner plate. Ladle the wine sauce around the leeks, about 2 tablespoons. Place a paupiette of sea bass on top of the leeks and garnish with a small sprig of thyme. Scatter the minced chives around the edges.

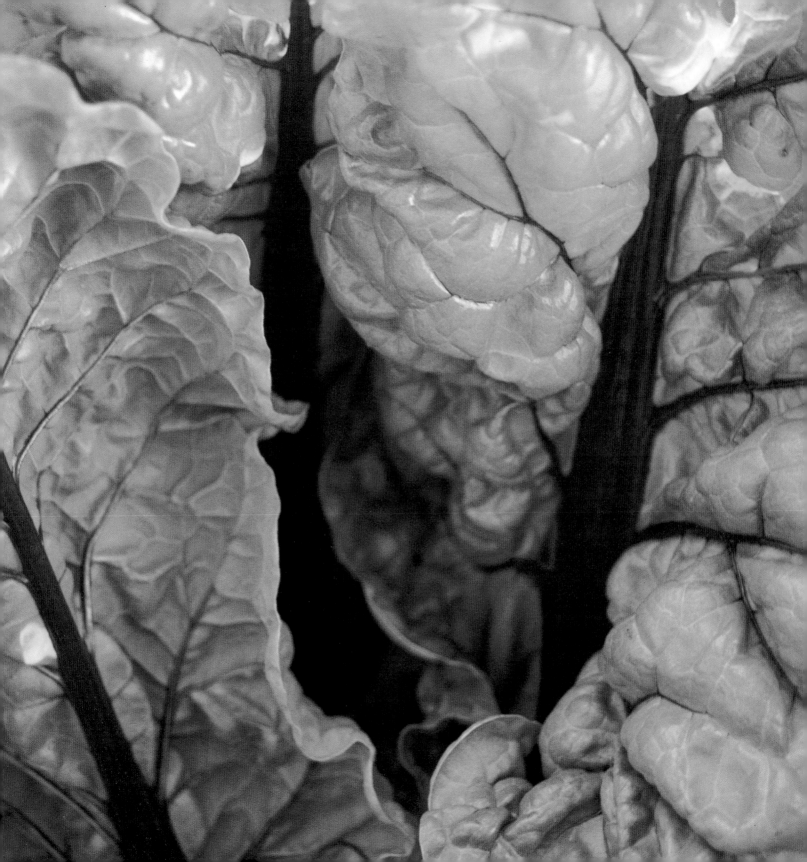

Yannick Cam

Provence
Washington, D.C.

 annick Cam was born in 1948 in a picturesque castle in Concarneau, France. He did not aspire to a life in the kitchen, but when he was 15, his father insisted that he take a summer job at a highly esteemed local restaurant. He found that he enjoyed the challenges of the competitive atmosphere and decided to stay on and apprentice with the chef. Doing so changed the course of his life.

During the next nine years, Yannick worked in several fine restaurants around France, culminating in a position at Laserre in Paris, a Michelin three-star restaurant. In 1972, he moved to New York, where he worked at The Four Seasons until he opened his first restaurant, Le Coup de Fusil, in 1977. It was often called the first contemporary French restaurant in America, and Yannick's use of fresh ingredients coupled with his unique style made it an instant success with both critics and diners.

He moved to Washington, D.C. in 1978 and opened Le Pavillon, which he operated for 14 years. His personal interpretation of classic French recipes and the elegant service in the dining room brought much attention and praise from the national press, including publications such as *Elle* and *Town and Country*. After closing Le Pavillon in 1992, he took his formidable skills to Restaurant Yannick in the Radisson Hotel.

In partnership with Savino Recine, he opened Coco Loco in Washington, D. C., in April 1994, followed five months later by the opening of Provence. Coco Loco is a churrasquería and tapas bar based on the Spanish concept of small tastes of food, but with decidedly Latin American flavors. Provence, with its elegant southern French atmosphere, is a world away from Coco Loco. Here the sunny flavors of the South of France are presented in the ambience of a seaside Mediterranean inn. Yannick describes the menu as a reassessment of traditional Provençal dishes. As a Frenchman he had some familiarity with the cuisine of the region, but he studied its history and traditions in depth in order to build a solid foundation of authenticity. In 1995 he was nominated for the James Beard Award for Best American Chef: Mid-Atlantic, for his excellence at both restaurants.

PROVENÇAL BRAISED RABBIT

Serves 4

With its lusty aromas of wine, olives and herbs, this rustic stew will transport you to the Mediterranean. Enjoy it with some crusty bread and a glass of Pinot Noir. To round out the menu serve a mesclun salad with goat cheese. For dessert, an almond tart and some fresh figs.

INGREDIENTS

3/4 cup olive oil (1/4 cup to sauté rabbit, 1/4 cup to sauté vegetables and 1/4 cup to sauté garlic and herbs)

1-1/2 pounds boneless rabbit meat

3/4 cup salt pork, diced

1-1/2 cups onions, diced

1 cup carrots, diced

1 cup celery, diced

2 tablespoons tomato paste

2 cups whole olives, rinsed with water and drained (Provençal olives are ideal, but other good Mediterranean or California olives would also be delicious)

6 cups dry red wine

1 calf's foot or 2-inch piece of beef shank (if these are difficult to find they can be omitted)

1-1/2 cups veal demi-glace or rich veal or chicken stock

3 to 4 large cloves garlic

4 bay leaves

1 tablespoon rosemary, roughly chopped

1/4 cup parsley, leaves only, roughly chopped

1 3-inch strip of orange peel, 1/2-inch wide

1 3-inch strip of lemon peel, 1/2-inch wide

Heat 1/4 cup olive oil in a sauté pan. Add rabbit pieces and cook until browned on the outside but still medium rare, about 10 minutes. Reserve the browned rabbit pieces on a platter while you prepare the braising liquid.

In a large flameproof casserole, heat 1/4 cup of the olive oil. Add the salt pork and cook over medium heat, stirring often, for about 5 minutes. Add the onions, carrots and celery and cook, stirring, for about 5 minutes. Add the tomato paste and cook for about 15 minutes, stirring, until slightly caramelized. Add the olives and red wine and simmer over medium heat for 15 minutes. At this point add the rabbit, the calf's foot or beef shank, and the demi-glace or stock. Braise over low heat for 45 minutes.

About 10 minutes before the braised rabbit is finished cooking, warm the last 1/4 cup olive oil in a small sauté pan. Add the garlic, herbs and citrus peel and sauté for about 5 minutes. Stir the herb mixture into the casserole and cook for another 5 minutes to blend the flavors.

This hearty dish can be made the day before and refrigerated. Reheat slowly over low heat until it is heated all the way through.

Robert Del Grande

Café Annie
Houston

Robert Del Grande grew up in San Francisco, California. Other than an affinity for cooking that was nurtured by his Italian grandmother and a summer job at a local ice cream parlor, there was nothing in his early years to predict his eventual success in the restaurant business. Instead, he pursued an academic career, receiving his B.S. in chemistry and biology at the University of San Francisco and his Ph.D. in biochemistry from the University of California at Riverside. Even while studying science, however, he had two experiences that would prove seminal: for four years he cooked for his graduate school roommates in exchange for their doing the dishes, and he fell in love with a library sciences student with family in Texas.

In 1991, while visiting his future wife, Mimi, in Houston, he was asked to help out in a family crisis. Her sister and brother-in-law had a small French restaurant, Café Annie. Their chef had walked out, so Robert volunteered to work in the kitchen until a replacement could be found. With no formal training, he approached the task like the scholar he was, reading everything he could get his hands on about the basics of French technique. He particularly liked the work of the Troisgros brothers and learned all the recipes in their cookbook. He also became fascinated with indigenous Texas cooking and began to experiment with Mexican ingredients while cooking meals for the staff. Robert's dishes were intuitive and creative, with bold flavors in intriguing combinations of spicy, smoky, sweet and hot. The menu evolved away from Nouvelle Cuisine to the cutting edge of contemporary Southwestern cooking. Robert and Mimi married, became partners in Café Annie and never looked back. In 1989 the restaurant moved from its first home in a small strip mall to more spacious and dramatic quarters in the Galleria district of Houston. In 1992, the partners opened Rio Ranch, a casual bistro featuring flawless home cooking.

The awards that Robert Del Grande and Café Annie have received are literally too numerous to list here. Some of the highlights are the James Beard Award for Outstanding Chef in 1992, an Ivy Award in 1992, the Fine Dining Hall of Fame, a DiRoNA award, Who's Who of Cooking in America, and *Food and Wine's* Honor Roll of American Chefs. He has appeared with Pierre Franey on PBS's *Great Chefs* series and with Julia Child in *Cooking with Master Chefs,* also on PBS.

CINNAMON ROASTED CHICKEN
WITH POZOLE AND PEARS

Serves 4

INGREDIENTS

2 chicken breasts

2 chicken legs (drumstick and thigh connected)

2 tablespoons good olive oil

1 teaspoon ground cinnamon

1 teaspoon brown sugar

1 teaspoon coarse salt

1/2 teaspoon freshly ground black pepper

1/2 large yellow onion, roughly chopped

4 cloves garlic

3 green pears, such as Bartlett or Anjou,
    not quite ripe

2 slices smoked bacon

3 cups chicken stock, preferably homemade

2 cups cooked pozole, or 1 29-ounce can of hominy

4 teaspoons dried cherries (optional)

1 tablespoon fresh herbs (thyme, chervil, rosemary
    and parsley), finely minced

1 tablespoon unsalted butter

Preheat the oven to 400 degrees. Rub the chicken pieces with olive oil. Combine the cinnamon, brown sugar, salt and pepper. Rub the chicken pieces with the cinnamon mixture. Arrange the chicken pieces in a roasting pan skin side up. Put the chicken into the oven and immediately lower the heat to 300

degrees and roast for 45 minutes. Baste the chicken with the pan juices and continue to roast it for an additional 30 minutes, or until the juices run clear.

Meanwhile, cut the onion and garlic into medium dice. Peel and core the pears and cut them into medium dice. Roughly chop the bacon. Combine the chopped onion, garlic, pears and bacon in a roasting pan just large enough to hold the ingredients in a single layer. Roast in the same oven as the chicken for the same amount of time. The ingredients should be well roasted and lightly caramelized. When the chicken is done, remove it from the oven and baste again. Allow it to rest in a warm place.

Transfer the roasted onion and pear mixture to a deep saucepan. Deglaze the roasting pan with the chicken stock and add it to the saucepan. Add the cooked pozole and bring the liquid to a boil. Add the dried cherries, if desired. Lower the heat to a simmer. Just before serving, add the herbs and whisk in the butter.

To serve, place a piece of chicken in the center of each of 4 deep dinner plates or shallow bowls. Spoon the pozole mixture and broth over the chicken.

KASPAR DONIER

KASPAR'S
SEATTLE

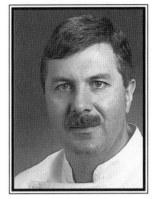

native of Switzerland, Kaspar Donier began his formal training at 16 as an apprentice at the Zurich Hilton. He worked at five-star restaurants in St. Moritz and Lausanne before moving to Vancouver, British Columbia in 1976. At the Hotel Vancouver, Kaspar was chef garde-manger and chef saucier; he then moved to the Four Seasons Hotel, where he served as sous-chef and executive sous-chef. In 1985, he was transferred to Houston's Inn on the Park, another Four Seasons property, and was promoted to executive chef the following year.

Kaspar and his wife Nancy returned to the Northwest in 1989 to open Kaspar's in Seattle. The menu reflects many years of work and travel in Europe, Canada and the United States, combined with the freshest Northwest seafood and produce. Every year since opening, Kaspar's has been listed as one of Seattle's Top Ten Restaurants. In 1994, the restaurant was awarded the only four-star review in *The Seattle Times* and was named Best Restaurant of the Year. Kaspar's has also been singled out as a top regional restaurant by *Gourmet, Bon Appétit, USA Today, Money* and *The New York Times*. In 1995 Kaspar was the national winner of the *Gourmet*/Evian Healthy Menu Award. For the past four years Kaspar has had the honor of being nominated for the James Beard Award for Best American Chef: Pacific Northwest. He has also been featured on the *Great Chefs* series on PBS and on Jeff Smith's *The Frugal Gourmet*.

The Doniers give generously back to the Seattle community through their support of many arts groups and charities, particularly the Seattle Food Lifeline and End Hunger networks, which help feed the homeless. Kaspar also enjoys teaching, giving cooking classes in the restaurant's kitchen and sharing his expertise with a steady flow of apprentices.

Goat Cheese Wrapped in Grape Leaves with Wine Braised Garlic

Serves 4

Kaspar's recipe could be either a rich and rustic first course or a striking element of an hors d'oeuvres buffet. We liked the look of partially opening the goat cheese packages and drizzling a little of the sauce over the cheese. Be sure to provide lots of crusty bread for dipping and spreading.

Ingredients

12 ounces fresh goat cheese, such as Montrachet
    (use a local goat cheese if available)

Freshly ground black pepper

8 large grape leaves, ideally tender young fresh ones
    (you may substitute the type that come in a jar
    preserved in brine, rinse and pat dry)

28 large garlic cloves, peeled

1-1/2 cups dry red wine

1/2 teaspoon salt

1/4 teaspoon freshly ground black pepper

2 tablespoons unsalted butter

1 medium sprig fresh rosemary, plus
    additional for garnish

Preheat oven to 375 degrees. Divide the goat cheese into 4 3-ounce portions and form into balls. Lightly coat the outside with freshly ground black pepper. Lay 2 grape leaves on your work surface with the stem ends overlapping. Center the goat cheese ball and wrap the leaves up and over the top. Flatten slightly with the palm of your hand to make a 2-inch patty. Repeat with the other 3 pieces of cheese. Refrigerate cheese while you make the garlic and wine sauce.

Place the peeled garlic, wine, salt, pepper, butter and rosemary into a heavy, medium-size stainless steel saucepan. Bring to a boil, then lower heat and simmer for 30 minutes or so, until garlic is soft and the liquid is reduced to a syrupy consistency. Remove rosemary sprig.

Place the wrapped goat cheeses in a nonstick pan and heat in the oven for 5 minutes, or until warmed through.

To serve, place each piece in the center of a deep plate or shallow soup bowl. Spoon the garlic cloves and sauce around. Garnish with sprigs of rosemary.

TODD ENGLISH

OLIVES
BOSTON

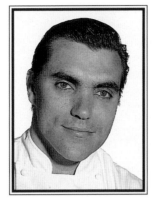

*T*odd English grew up in Texas, dreaming of a future as a major league catcher. At some undetermined moment while he was in college in North Carolina, cooking overcame baseball as his primary passion. At 20, he enrolled in the Culinary Institute of America, from which he graduated with honors. He continued his studies with Jean-Jacques Rachou in the kitchen of Manhattan's La Côte Basque, then went to Italy, where he apprenticed at Dal Pescatore in Canto Sull Olio and Paraccuchi in Locando D'Angelo. It was in Italy that Todd developed his appreciation of the intensely flavored rustic food of the Mediterranean countryside. Upon returning to America, he was executive chef of the award-winning Northern Italian restaurant Michela's for three years.

In 1989, Todd and his wife Olivia opened Olives in Charlestown, an historic section of Boston. Their 50-seat storefront restaurant soon attracted national and international attention for its simple and lusty dishes prepared in an open kitchen with a wood-fired grill, rotisserie and ovens. Olives has since moved to a larger dining room, and the original Olives location is occupied by their more casual pizzeria, Figs. Another Figs was recently opened in Boston.

Olives was voted Best New Restaurant by *Boston* magazine and one of the nation's Top Ten Restaurants by *Esquire*. It has also been featured in articles in *Bon Appétit, The New York Times, Food & Wine, Art Culinaire* and *Food Arts*. The kitchen in Todd and Olivia's home has been the subject of articles in *Food & Wine* and *Home*. In the spring of 1994, Todd was named Best American Chef: Northeast by The James Beard Foundation and received the first Robert Mondavi Award for Culinary Excellence. He can be seen on the *America's Rising Star Chefs* television series now airing on PBS and on the Discovery Channel's *Great Chefs of the Northeast* series. Todd is currently working on a cookbook, *Olives' Kitchen*, scheduled to be published in the fall of 1996.

STRACOTTO OF SALMON
BRAISED IN RED WINE

Serves 4

Todd sent the following note about the history of his recipe: *"I have always said that I think fish, especially salmon, goes extremely well with Pinot Noir. This is an adaptation from an ancient Italian dish, Stracotto di Cavallo, where horsemeat was braised for a long period of time in an aromatic broth using the local red wine. When tender, the meat was removed and the vegetables were puréed with the broth. This became the sauce for the dish. In this salmon recipe, I have adapted the cooking technique but maintained the concept. Polenta is served with the dish, just as it was traditionally."*

INGREDIENTS

BRAISED SALMON

4 6- to 8-ounce salmon steaks

1 onion, roughly chopped

2 medium carrots, roughly chopped

3 stalks of celery, roughly chopped

1 leek, white part only, roughly chopped

2 cloves of garlic, peeled and roughly chopped

1 medium sprig rosemary

1 cinnamon stick

2 bottles dry red wine

2 bay leaves

1/2 pound smoked slab bacon, finely diced

4 cloves, wrapped in a cheesecloth bag

3 tablespoons butter

1 teaspoon salt

1/2 teaspoon freshly ground pepper

Sprigs of rosemary and Italian parsley for garnish

POLENTA

6 cups water

1-1/2 cups stoneground cornmeal

1/4 cup heavy cream

4 tablespoons butter

1/4 cup grated parmesan

1-1/2 tablespoons salt

1/2 tablespoon freshly ground black pepper

1/4 cup mascarpone cheese

Place the salmon steaks in a ceramic or glass dish large enough to hold them in one layer. Strew all of the other ingredients (except the butter, salt and pepper) over and around the salmon. Pour the wine over all and marinate, refrigerated, for at least 3 hours.

Remove the salmon from the marinade and reserve, refrigerated. Pour the marinade into a large stainless steel pot, ideally large enough to eventually hold the salmon steaks in one layer. Bring the marinade to a simmer, but do not allow it to boil. Slowly reduce marinade by half. This will take approximately an hour so an ideal time to start the polenta (see instructions below) would be when the reduction is at the halfway point. Season the reserved salmon steaks generously with salt and pepper. When the simmering wine mixture has reduced, add the salmon steaks and poach for about 12 minutes. Carefully remove the salmon from the pot and set aside in a warm place.

Remove the cinnamon stick and cloves from the pot and discard. Pass the wine and vegetable mixture through a food mill, or purée in a blender. Pour the purée back into the pot and bring to a boil. Stir in the butter.

To prepare the polenta, bring the water to boil in a large heavy saucepan. Stir in the cornmeal using a whisk to prevent lumps from forming. Switch to a wooden spoon and continue to stir for another few minutes. Turn the heat down to the point that the polenta is just bubbling gently. Cook another 20 to 25 minutes, stirring occasionally. Remove from the heat and stir in the heavy cream, mascarpone and parmesan.

To serve, put 2 large spoonfuls of polenta in the center of a deep dinner plate or a shallow soup bowl. Place the salmon steak on top of the polenta and ladle the sauce over the top and all around it. Garnish with sprigs of rosemary and Italian parsley.

DEAN FEARING

THE MANSION ON TURTLE CREEK
DALLAS

*D*ean Fearing was a guitar-strumming, 23-year-old who worked nights burning steaks in a Holiday Inn when he enrolled in a class that brought his aspirations into clear focus. It was a community college course taught by a retired chef in Louisville that turned the trick. He subsequently attended the Culinary Institute of America to study classical technique, graduating in 1978. He began his career in Cincinnati at Maisonette, followed by The Pyramid Room at The Fairmount Hotel in Dallas. When The Mansion on Turtle Creek opened its doors in 1980, Dean came to the restaurant as executive sous-chef, a position he resigned to become chef and part owner of Agnew's. There his daring experiments with products and recipes indigenous to the Southwest drew the attention of Craig Claiborne, the influential food editor of *The New York Times*. This marked the beginning of Dean's rise to international prominence.

In 1985, Dean returned to The Mansion on Turtle Creek as executive chef. More than a decade later, he continues to garner the top awards in his profession. In 1994, he won The James Beard Foundation's Award as Best American Chef: Southwest, and in 1996, the restaurant at The Mansion on Turtle Creek received its fifth star from the Mobil Guide. Dean has been featured in numerous articles in the nation's food and wine press and is the author of two cookbooks, *The Mansion on Turtle Creek Cookbook* and *Dean Fearing's Southwest Cuisine: Blending Asia and the Americas*. At this writing he can be seen demonstrating some of his signature Southwest recipes on PBS's *Cooking with Master Chefs* series with Julia Child.

This all-American chef, who still plays guitar and wears flashy cowboy boots, sees his career as similar to those of the master chefs of France. "It is typical," he says, "for a master chef to work at the same restaurant for 30 years, where his fortune is intertwined with that of the restaurant. I expect to be at The Mansion for at least 20 more years."

Molasses Duck
with Smoked Vegetable Dressing
and Peach Chutney

Serves 4

Dean's recipe is a delectable twist on the classic Southern combination of poultry with cornbread stuffing.

Ingredients

Molasses Duck

2 whole ducks, approximately 5 pounds each

Salt and freshly ground black pepper

1-1/2 cups molasses

2 tablespoons Tabasco sauce

2 teaspoons finely grated ginger

2 teaspoons finely minced garlic

Smoked Vegetable Dressing

2 medium yellow onions, diced medium

2 stalks of celery, diced medium

2 medium carrots, diced medium

1 red bell pepper, seeds and membrane removed, diced medium

1 tablespoon olive oil

1 tablespoon chopped fresh sage or 1 teaspoon dried sage

2 teaspoons chopped fresh thyme or 3/4 teaspoon dried thyme

3 cups cornbread crumbs

2 cups good quality white bread cut into1/2-inch cubes

1-1/2 cups rich chicken stock

Salt and freshly ground pepper to taste

Peach Chutney

5 ripe peaches

1 tablespoon finely diced ginger,

1 tablespoon sugar

1 teaspoon ground cinnamon

2 teaspoons lemon juice

Preheat oven to 325 degrees. Rinse each duck with cool water and pat dry. Season inside and out with salt and freshly ground pepper. Place ducks on a rack in a large roasting pan and roast for 2 hours. While the duck is cooking make the molasses glaze. In a medium bowl, combine the molasses, Tabasco sauce, ginger and garlic. Stir and set aside. After the duck has roasted for 2 hours, remove the pan from the oven and drain all of the fat out of the pan and discard. Brush the molasses glaze over the entire surface of each duck and return them to the oven. Baste the ducks with the molasses glaze every 8 minutes for 40 minutes. The ducks' skin should be crisp and mahogany-colored.

While the duck is roasting, prepare the smoked vegetable dressing. Place onions, celery, carrots and red bell pepper in a smoker and cold smoke for 15 to 20 minutes. (See NOTE below.) Remove. Heat oil in a large sauté pan over medium heat. Add smoked vegetables and sauté for 5 minutes or until the onions are transparent and the carrots are soft. Add sage and thyme and sauté for another minute. Add cornbread and white bread and stir to combine. Slowly add the chicken stock, stirring gently, until dressing has enough moisture to come together but is not soggy. Season with salt and pepper and keep warm.

To make the peach chutney, peel and pit the peaches. Cut 3 of them into medium dice, sprinkle with a little lemon juice and set aside. Purée the remaining peaches in a blender. Pour the purée into a medium stainless steel saucepan with the ginger, sugar, cinnamon and lemon juice. Reduce the mixture over medium heat, stirring occasionally, until thick. This should take about 5 or 6 minutes. Add the diced peaches to the saucepan and cook, stirring occasionally, until mixture is heated through. The chutney can be made ahead and reheated just before serving time.

To serve, remove the ducks from oven. Carefully lift each duck from the roasting pan and place on a cutting board. As soon as the ducks are cool enough to handle, cut the breasts away from the bone, disturbing the molasses-glazed skin as little as possible. Cut the legs off by severing at the hip joint. Spoon a portion of the Smoked Vegetable Dressing in the middle of each warm dinner plate. Place a duck breast and leg next to the dressing and spoon a portion of Peach Chutney over each duck breast.

NOTE: *If you don't have a smoker, you can create your own stovetop version with a wok. First, soak a handful of wood chips in warm water for 10 minutes (we particularly like fruitwood, such as cherry or apple, with this recipe). Drain. Line a wok with aluminum foil. Put half a cup of rice in the bottom and set over high heat. When the rice begins to smolder, add the wood chips. Meanwhile, make a shallow basket out of foil and put the vegetables in it. Set a round cake rack in the wok so that it rests above the smoking chips. Set the foil basket on the rack, allowing plenty of room for the smoke to circulate. Cover the wok tightly, turn the burner off, and allow the vegetables to smoke for 15 to 20 minutes.*

Rack of Lamb on Pear Purée
with Blue Cheese Bread Pudding
and Port Wine Sauce

Serves 4

Ingredients

1 tablespoon vegetable oil

2 8-rib racks of lamb (have your butcher French cut them for you)

Salt and pepper to taste

Sprigs of fresh thyme or Italian parsley for garnish

Pear Purée

4 medium Bartlett or Anjou pears

1/2 cup white Port wine

1/2 cup chicken stock

1 tablespoon fresh ginger, grated

1/2 teaspoon unsalted butter

Salt and lemon juice to taste

Port Wine Sauce

1 tablespoon vegetable oil

1 medium yellow onion, chopped

1 stalk celery, chopped

1/2 medium carrot, chopped

2 shallots, peeled and chopped

2 cloves of garlic, peeled and chopped

1 cup Port wine

1 sprig fresh thyme

1 tablespoon coarsely ground black pepper

1 cup veal demi-glace or rich veal or chicken stock

Salt and lemon juice to taste

Blue Cheese Bread Pudding

Butter for coating ramekins

1 French bread baguette

1/2 cup blue cheese, crumbled

3 eggs

1 cup whipping cream

1 shallot, minced

1 clove garlic, minced

Salt and white pepper to taste

Season the lamb with salt and pepper and set aside, refrigerated.

To prepare the pear purée, roughly chop pears into 1-inch pieces. Put the pears, wine, chicken broth and ginger in a medium stainless steel saucepan and simmer until pears are soft, about 20 minutes. Purée the mixture in a blender or food processor until smooth, adding the butter at the end. Season with salt and lemon juice and hold in a warm spot.

To prepare the Port wine sauce, heat the oil in a heavy saucepan. Sauté the onion, celery and carrots until golden brown. Add shallots and garlic and cook about 1 more minute. Add the Port wine, bring to a boil and reduce by half. Add the pepper, thyme and veal demi-glace or stock. Simmer the sauce about 30 minutes, then strain it through a fine sieve. Season with salt and lemon to taste.

Preheat the oven to 350 degrees. To prepare the blue cheese bread pudding, butter small individual ceramic ramekins or soufflé dishes. Slice baguette into 1/4-inch slices. Place a slice of bread in the bottom of the ramekin, then sprinkle some blue cheese on top, alternating bread and cheese until almost full. Be sure to press down tightly after each layer. Combine eggs and cream with garlic, shallots, salt and white pepper to taste. Whisk mixture until smooth. Pour over the bread and cheese and let it soak in for about 5 minutes. You may need to add more of the mixture as it is absorbed. Place the ramekins in an ovenproof pan. Pour hot water into the pan until it reaches a level about 2/3 up the side of the ramekins. Bake for about 15 to 20 minutes, or until custards are puffy and golden brown on top. Remove ramekins from water bath and let rest for at least 5 minutes before unmolding. Keep them warm until time to serve.

Raise oven temperature to 400 degrees. Heat oil in a heavy flameproof roasting pan. Over high heat, sear the meat until browned, about 3 minutes. Place lamb in oven to roast until medium rare, about 12 minutes, or until its internal temperature reaches 130 degrees.

For each serving, place a generous spoonful of pear purée slightly off-center on a large dinner plate. Carve the lamb rack into chops and arrange them, slightly overlapping, on top of the purée. Unmold the bread pudding and place to the side. Sauce the chops generously and garnish with a sprig of fresh thyme or Italian parsley.

JOYCE GOLDSTEIN

SQUARE ONE
SAN FRANCISCO

*F*ood and art have been the lifelong passions of Joyce Goldstein. After an auspicious academic career—she graduated magna cum laude and Phi Beta Kappa from Smith College and earned an M.F.A. from the Yale School of Art and Architecture—she moved to San Francisco to paint. In the '60s and '70s, while raising her children, she exhibited her paintings and founded the California Street Cooking School. At the cooking school she directed the curriculum and taught both the technique and the history of various ethnic cuisines. In 1980 she began teaching kitchen design at the University of California's School of Architecture in Berkeley and became involved in cooking at Chez Panisse Café. Before long she was chef and manager, positions she held for several years. In 1983, inspired by her experience at Chez Panisse, Joyce opened her own superb restaurant in San Francisco, Square One.

In addition to overseeing all aspects of Square One, Joyce has found time to write many cookbooks. In 1989, she published *The Mediterranean Kitchen*, a detailed culinary tour of the regions bordering the Mediterranean, including North Africa and the Middle East.

Her second book, *Back to Square One*, came out in 1992 and won both the Julia Child and James Beard Awards as Best General Cookbook of that year. In partnership with Chuck Williams she won another James Beard Award, for Best Entertaining Book, in 1993. In addition to that book, *Festive Occasions*, she has also teamed up with Chuck Williams for *Casual Occasions* (1995) and two Williams-Sonoma Kitchen Library books: *Beef* and *Fish* (1992). Her *Mediterranean The Beautiful* was published in 1994 by HarperCollins, and she has two more books on the horizon for 1996.

Joyce received the James Beard Award for Best American Chef: California in 1993. A founding member of the board of directors of the International Association of Women Chefs and Restaurateurs, she is also on the board of both Meals on Wheels and Open Hand. Joyce donates an extraordinary amount of her time and energy to community affairs and numerous charitable causes. She has passed her enthusiasm for food and wine on to her son Evan Goldstein, a master sommelier, and she has high hopes that her new granddaughter, Elena, will carry on the family tradition.

Grilled Chicken
in a Pomegranate Marinade

Serves 4

The sweet and tart flavors of the pomegranate marinade make a wonderful crisp glaze on the chicken. It is best to keep the skin on the bird, otherwise the meat will toughen while cooking.

Ingredients

2 pounds boneless chicken breasts or thighs, or
    combination of the two, with skin on

Marinade

1 small onion, grated

2 large cloves garlic, minced

1/2 cup pomegranate syrup or molasses
    (Pomegranate syrup can be found in specialty
    food stores. Do not substitute grenadine syrup,
    which is much sweeter.)

1/4 cup dry red wine

1-1/2 teaspoons ground coriander

1-1/2 teaspoons freshly ground black pepper

1/4 teaspoon ground cloves

Pinch cayenne

1/2 teaspoon salt

3 tablespoons chopped cilantro

Put the chicken in a nonreactive container, such as a glass or ceramic baking dish. Combine all of the marinade ingredients and pour over the chicken. Cover and marinate in the refrigerator for 6 hours, or overnight.

Make a charcoal fire or preheat broiler. Broil or grill chicken for about 5 minutes on each side for breasts, a little longer for thighs.

Serve with couscous or a cracked wheat pilaf tossed with chopped cilantro, green onions and toasted walnuts. Start the meal with a salad of oranges, red onions and olives and finish with honey ice cream and date bars.

Moroccan-Style Roast Fish
with Caramelized Onions and Raisins

Serves 4

Ingredients

4 6- to 7-ounce fish filets (sea bass, red snapper
    or rock cod would be good choices)

Salt

4 tablespoons olive oil

4 large onions, sliced

1 teaspoon ground cinnamon

2 teaspoons ground cumin

1/2 teaspoon ground ginger

1 tablespoon grated orange zest

Salt and freshly ground pepper to taste

1 cup raisins soaked in a little orange
    juice until plump

2 to 3 tablespoons mild honey to taste

Optional: a little lemon juice, if needed for balance

1/2 cup toasted walnut pieces for garnish

Charmoula Spice Paste

1/2 teaspoon freshly ground black pepper

1/2 teaspoon ground cinnamon

1/2 teaspoon ground ginger

1 teaspoon ground cumin

1/4 teaspoon crushed saffron threads
    steeped in 1/8 cup of water

Enough olive oil to make a paste

Lightly salt fish filets and rub liberally with the charmoula spice paste (see recipe). Marinate in the refrigerator for 2 to 3 hours.

Heat the olive oil in a large sauté pan. Add the onions, salt lightly, and sauté until very tender, about 15 minutes. Add the spices and orange zest and cook until the onions are caramelized. Season with salt and pepper. Stir in the raisins. Add the honey, then taste for seasoning, adding salt and pepper and the lemon juice if needed. Simmer for 5 minutes to blend flavors.

Preheat the oven to 450 degrees. Place the fish filets on an oiled baking pan, cover with the caramelized onion mixture and bake until the fish is fork tender, 8 to 12 minutes depending on the thickness of the fish.

To serve, sprinkle the fish with toasted walnuts and serve with couscous and sautéed spinach.

Jean Joho

Everest
Chicago

*J*ean Joho's interest in food and cooking began when he was a child in Alsace. He started working at the age of 13, washing vegetables and peeling potatoes in Paul Haeberlin's kitchen at the three-star Auberge de L'Ill. He attended the École Hôtelière in Strasbourg where he studied the hotel and restaurant business, and specialized in pastry, cheesemaking and wine. His training continued in restaurants throughout France and Switzerland, and by age 23 he was the chef of a first-class restaurant with a staff of 35. In 1984, Jean was hired to open a Maxim's in Chicago. It was there that he met Richard Melman of Lettuce Entertain You Enterprises and began a long and successful collaboration.

Everest was opened in 1984 on the 40th floor of the LaSalle Building in Chicago, making it a pinnacle on both the skyline and the culinary scene. Jean has been named one of the nation's top chefs by many publications, including *Food & Wine, Bon Appétit, Esquire* and *Playboy,* as well as the Chicago press. He was honored with the 1995 James Beard Award for Best American Chef: Midwest, was named Best Chef in the Midwest by the Fine Beverage and Food Federation in 1994, and was voted Best Chef and Best Restaurant in *Chicago* magazine's 1994 survey. The Zagat and Mobil guidebooks and *Maîtres-Cuisiniers de France* have all given Everest their highest ratings for its impeccable cuisine and outstanding wine cellar.

In 1995, Jean Joho opened Brasserie Jo, Chicago's first authentic brasserie. For the grand 7,000-square-foot dining space, he drew upon his Alsatian background to create a menu and environment in a casual and lighthearted style. Another of his enterprises is the Corner Bakery, which bakes all of the breads for Brasserie Jo and also has five retail locations. Since 1992, Jean has been a vice president and operating officer of Lettuce Entertain You Enterprises.

Cured Duck Salad with Mixed Baby Greens and Walnut Vinaigrette

Serves 4

You will need to start this recipe eight days in advance to give the duck breasts time to cure. This simple curing technique is used in the traditional cooking of the southwestern part of France. The rich flavors of the duck and nuts are balanced by the greens, making this a delightful salad for a fall luncheon or supper.

Ingredients

2 large boneless duck breasts

1 tablespoon kosher salt

2 teaspoons black peppercorns, crushed

Leaves from 4 sprigs of fresh thyme

4 loosely filled cups of beautiful small mixed salad
    leaves, with a good portion of frisée or other
    slightly bitter greens

1 tablespoon fruity red wine vinegar or
    berry vinegar

1 shallot, finely minced

3 tablespoons walnut oil

Salt and freshly ground pepper

1 tablespoon toasted and crushed hazelnuts

1 tablespoon almond slices, lightly toasted

Place the duck breasts flesh side down on your work surface. With a very sharp knife, slice off the skin, trying to leave a thin coating of fat still attached to the meat. Take the skin you have removed and roll it up tightly. Wrap the roll in plastic wrap, tie with string and freeze. This will become curly cracklings for the final preparation.

Rub the duck breasts with the salt, pepper and thyme, patting the mixture on to coat. Put the duck breasts in a single layer in a ceramic or glass container and refrigerate for 12 hours to begin the curing process. After 12 hours, turn the breasts and refrigerate for another 12 hours.

Remove the duck breasts from the refrigerator. Wipe each breast dry and wrap in 3 or 4 layers of clean, dry cheesecloth. Tie each end tightly with string and suspend the duck breasts in a cool, dry room with good circulation, but no draft. The ideal temperature would be about 60 degrees. It will take about 7 days to air-dry the duck breasts. When cured, they will have the color and texture of a prosciutto ham.

Just before you plan to serve the salad, turn on the broiler to preheat. Remove the duck skin from the freezer. Slice it crosswise into fine slivers, then place on a baking sheet and broil until crispy and golden. Drain the cracklings on paper towels.

Make a simple vinaigrette, whisking the walnut oil into the vinegar and shallots and seasoning with salt and pepper.

Slice the duck "hams" into very thin slices, crosswise on a slight bias. Arrange the slices in a rosette shape around the edges of 4 individual plates. Toss the salad greens with the vinaigrette and arrange in a mound in the middle of each plate. Sprinkle with the cracklings, the hazelnuts and the almond slices and serve.

❖

EMERIL LAGASSE

EMERIL'S
NEW ORLEANS

*A*ll through high school in Fall River, Massachusetts, Emeril Lagasse worked part time at a Portuguese bakery, where he became expert in the art of bread and pastrymaking. When he graduated he passed up a music scholarship to begin working his way through the culinary program at Johnson and Wales University, from which he eventually earned his doctorate. After finishing his formal education, he polished his skills in the kitchens of Paris and Lyons, then returned to work in restaurants in New York, Boston and Philadelphia. In 1982, he caught the attention of the doyenne of New Orleans' restaurant community, Ella Brennan, who persuaded the 26-year-old prodigy to take the position of executive chef at the legendary Commander's Palace.

After seven years at Commander's Palace, he opened his own restaurant, Emeril's. The menu is creative and eclectic, described by Emeril as "New New Orleans" cuisine: a pastiche of tempting dishes in the style of Southwestern, Pacific Rim or New England cooking, but always rooted in the Creole genre. His success was instantaneous and continues to grow. In 1990, *Esquire* named Emeril's Best New Restaurant of the Year, and in 1991 Emeril was named Best American Chef: Southeast by The James Beard Foundation. He was named one of the Top 25 Chefs in America by *Food & Wine*, received The Ivy Award from *Restaurants and Institutions* and been inducted into *Nation's Restaurant News'* Fine Dining Hall of Fame.

In 1993, Emeril opened Nola, his casual French Quarter bistro, and it, too, was honored by *Esquire* as The Best New Restaurant of the Year. His latest project is Emeril's New Orleans Fish House in the monumental MGM Grand Hotel in Las Vegas. His television series on TVFN called *The Essence of Emeril* has made him a national TV personality, and his first cookbook, *Emeril's New New Orleans Cooking*, was published in 1993 by William Morrow.

PINOT NOIR ZABAGLIONE WITH
RED GRAPES AND BLUE CHEESE

Serves 2

*Emeril's innovative recipe is a sublime blend of cheese course
and dessert—a perfect excuse for sipping wine to the very end
of the meal.*

INGREDIENTS

3 cups Pinot Noir

1/4 cup sugar, plus 1 teaspoon

2 egg yolks

Juice of a 1/2 lemon

Powdered sugar for dusting

6 ounces red seedless grapes, cut into 2 nice-looking
    clusters, washed and dried

1-1/2 ounces high quality blue-veined cheese, such
    as Roquefort, Oregon Blue or Maytag Blue, cut
    in thin slices

6 toast points cut from French bread, sliced
    1/2 inch thick

In a small sauce pan combine the Pinot Noir and
1/4 cup of the sugar. Over medium heat, reduce to
1/2 cup; this will take about half an hour. Set aside
to cool for 10 minutes. In a medium bowl, whisk
together the egg yolks, lemon juice and 1 teaspoon
sugar. Place the bowl over a pot of simmering water
and whisk until thick and pale. Slowly add all but
1 tablespoon of the cooled wine syrup. Continue
to whisk until the mixture is very thick and frothy.
The result is a Pinot Noir zabaglione. Set aside in
a warm place.

Line a small baking sheet with a piece of waxed
paper. Dust the grape clusters with powdered sugar.
Holding the cluster by the stem, dip the grapes into
the zabaglione mixture, completely coating them.
Place on the waxed paper and put in the freezer for
15 minutes, just long enough to set the zabaglione.

Meanwhile, drizzle the remaining red wine syrup in
decorative patterns on two large plates (make sure
they are at room temperature). Divide the blue
cheese and the toast points between the two plates,
arranging them around the edges. Take the grape
clusters from the freezer, place in the center of each
plate, and serve immediately.

GEORGE MAHAFFEY

THE LITTLE NELL
ASPEN

George Mahaffey grew up in Virginia, one of five children in a busy family with a workaday approach to food. He studied philosophy at Virginia Commonwealth University, where he received his B.A. with honors, then did graduate work in philosophy and mathematical logic at the University of Virginia. While a student he became interested in cooking as a means of relaxation and artistic expression and soon changed his career goals from the academic to the culinary. His formal training was through a three-year chef's apprenticeship program under the auspices of the American Culinary Federation. Following his certification, he gained additional experience at The Hotel Hershey in Pennsylvania and The Cloister on Sea Island, Georgia before accepting a position at The Hotel Bel Air in Los Angeles.

As executive chef of The Bel Air he received much acclaim, including a Chef of the Year award from the California Restaurant Writers Association in 1991. While at the prestigious hotel he authored a cookbook, *The Bel Air Book of Southern California Food and Entertaining*.

Although George enjoyed his work in Los Angeles, he began to look for a more serene setting in which to raise his five children. In 1992, he assumed executive chef responsibilities at The Little Nell, a Five-Star, Five-Diamond, Relais & Châteaux property at the base of Aspen's ski slopes. There he has developed a style of cooking he calls "American Alpine," using indigenous seasonal products from the Rocky Mountains overlaid with flavors from other cuisines. He meets the challenge of finding impeccable ingredients in a remote setting by working closely with local farmers, ranchers and gatherers of wild foods.

Under George's direction, the restaurant at The Little Nell has been a winner of the DiRoNA award, been named as one of the top ten restaurants in the United States by *Restaurants and Institutions* and is a recipient of the Ivy Award for 1996. He has received excellent reviews from numerous newspapers and magazines, including *Bon Appétit*, *Wine Spectator*, *Food Arts*, *Esquire* and *Food & Wine*. In 1994, George was nominated for The James Beard Foundation's Best American Chef: Southwest award.

PAN ROASTED RUBY TROUT
WITH SAUTÉED CÈPES, CREAMY LEEKS
AND GARLIC-THYME SAUCE

Serves 4

INGREDIENTS

2 ruby trout, about 1-1/4 pounds each, fileted

Olive oil and butter for cooking

GARLIC-THYME SAUCE

2 teaspoons unsalted butter

8 cloves of garlic, peeled and cut in half

2 tablespoons sliced shallot

2-1/2 cups chicken stock

2 tablespoons dry red wine

1 tablespoon soy sauce

1/2 teaspoon sambal oolek (Indonesian pepper
    sauce, which can be found in Asian markets
    or specialty food stores)

3 sprigs of fresh thyme

8 to 10 small cèpes (boletus mushrooms) about the
    size of a golf ball (or substitute large, firm
    cultivated mushrooms)

1 tablespoon unsalted butter

1 tablespoon chopped shallot

1 tablespoon chopped Italian parsley

1 tablespoon chopped chervil

3 large leeks, white part only, cut in half and
    thoroughly washed

1/2 cup heavy cream

Salt and freshly ground pepper

1-1/2 tablespoons thinly sliced scallions, cut on
    the bias

1 tablespoon chopped golden tomato
    (or substitute red tomato)

1 teaspoon chopped fresh thyme

1 tablespoon thinly sliced garlic cloves, blanched
    twice in fresh water, 5 minutes each time,
    then drained

16 of the smallest cherry tomatoes you can find,
    Sweet 100s or currant tomatoes would be ideal

Lay the trout filets on your work surface and trim
the ends of the filets on the bias. Cut each filet
in half on a sharp bias to produce a total of
8 approximately diamond-shaped pieces. Season
trout lightly with salt and freshly ground black
pepper and set aside, refrigerated, until time to
sauté them.

To prepare the sauce, melt the butter in a small stainless steel saucepan, add the garlic cloves and sauté until they are a light golden brown. Add the shallots and 1/2 cup of the chicken stock and, stirring occasionally, allow to reduce to a glaze. Add the red wine and another 1/2 cup chicken stock and reduce again completely. Add the soy sauce, sambal oolek and the remaining 1-1/2 cups chicken stock. Turn the heat down and simmer until reduced to 1 cup. Remove the thyme sprig and purée in a food processor or blender. Strain into a small saucepan and set aside until time to serve.

While the sauce is reducing, melt the butter in a small sauté pan over high heat. Add the mushrooms, shallots and herbs and cook until golden. Season with salt and pepper. Moisten the mixture with 2 tablespoons water. Stir, then set aside in a warm place.

Cut the cleaned and halved leeks into 3/8-inch pieces. Put the pieces of leek and the cream in a small pan. Cook over medium heat until the cream binds to the leeks. Remove from the heat, but keep cream mixture warm. This can be done while the sauce is reducing and the mushrooms are cooking.

Preheat the oven to 350 degrees. Just before you are ready to serve, heat a small amount of olive oil in a large ovenproof sauté pan that is large enough to hold all the filets in one layer, or use two smaller pans. Sear the fish, flesh side down, over high heat for about 2 minutes. Turn each filet and brush lightly with soft butter. Finish cooking in the oven, approximately 2 to 3 minutes.

While the trout is in the oven, reheat the sauce, adding the sliced scallions, chopped tomato, chopped thyme and blanched garlic slices. Add the cherry tomatoes to the mushroom mixture and stir to combine. In the center of each of four large heated dinner plates, spoon 2 to 3 tablespoons of warm creamed leeks. Place 2 pieces of trout filet on top, allowing the leeks to show. Spoon 2 to 3 tablespoons of the mushroom-tomato mixture over the top of the trout filets. Ladle a generous amount of the garlic-thyme sauce around the perimeter of the plate and serve immediately.

ROBERT MCGRATH

WINDOWS ON THE GREEN AT THE PHOENICIAN
SCOTTSDALE, ARIZONA

*R*obert McGrath, a native of Louisville, Kentucky, has always enjoyed traveling. After attending the Cordon Bleu Cooking School in Paris and the Culinary Institute of America he combined vocation and avocation with positions in Florida, California, New York and Texas. His 15 years of experience in the hospitality business includes roles as executive chef at the Plantation Yacht Harbor in the Florida Keys; sous-chef at the Disneyland Hotel in California; executive chef of the Arrowwood Resort in Westchester, New York; chef de cuisine at the Four Seasons Hotel in Austin, Texas; and executive chef of the Four Seasons Hotel in Houston. He was chef/proprietor of his own restaurant, Sierra, in Houston before coming to Windows on the Green at The Phoenician in 1993.

Robert's expertise and creativity have been recognized with a variety of awards and honors. In 1986, after winning gold medals in competitions around the country, he was named a member of the United States Culinary Team. He was singled out as one of the Ten Best New Chefs in America by *Food & Wine* in 1988. The following year, DeVille, the restaurant at the Houston Four Seasons over which he presided, was named one of The Best New Restaurants in America by *Esquire*. In 1990, his peers in the Chefs in America organization named him Chef of the Year and he was once again honored by *Esquire* when Sierra was named in its survey of The Best New Restaurants in America in 1992.

The *Gourmet*/Evian Healthy Menu Awards named Robert the Southwest regional winner in 1993 and the national winner in 1994. *Gourmet* featured him in its 1994 piece "Chefs Across America" and he was nominated as Best American Chef: Southwest in 1994 and 1995 by The James Beard Foundation.

The Phoenician is a luxury destination resort situated on 130 acres of lush desert terrain at the foot of Camelback Mountain. At Windows on the Green, Robert uses such regional ingredients as jicama, cactus, chiles and game along with the traditional techniques of smoking and grilling to create his innovative version of Southwest cuisine. In addition to his many duties at the restaurant, Robert has created a series of monthly cooking classes called Robert McGrath & Friends, with outstanding guest chefs from around the country.

Tenderloin of Beef
on a Blueberry Barbecue Sauce
with Roasted Garlic-Green Chile Mashed Potatoes

Serves 4

Robert's menu is ideal for a late summer cookout, when blueberries and garden vegetables are at their peak.

Ingredients

4 7-ounce beef tenderloin steaks
Kosher salt and fresh cracked black pepper

Roasted Garlic-Green Chile Mashed Potatoes

3 large russet potatoes, peeled and cut into
    1/2-inch cubes
2 tablespoons roasted garlic purée (about 2 heads
    of garlic)
2 tablespoons roasted green chile purée
    (roast and peel a fresh Anaheim chile pepper
    or use canned green chiles)
1/2 cup whole milk
1/4 cup butter
Salt and freshly ground pepper to taste

Blueberry Barbecue Sauce

    (makes about a pint)
1 tablespoon butter
1/4 cup finely chopped onions
1 tablespoon finely chopped jalapeño pepper
1 pint blueberries

3 tablespoons brown sugar
1/4 cup rice wine vinegar
1/4 cup tomato ketchup
3 tablespoons Dijon mustard
1 teaspoon Tabasco sauce
1/4 cup butter

Vegetable Garnish

1 tablespoon butter
1/4 cup blanched haricots verts (tiny green beans)
    or French-cut green beans
1/4 cup corn kernels
1/4 cup blanched fava beans, or other fresh
    shell beans
1 tablespoon diced red bell pepper
2 tablespoons diced red onion
Salt and freshly ground black pepper to taste

1/4 cup fresh blueberries for garnish

Season the steaks on both sides with salt and pepper and set aside in a cool place.

To prepare the mashed potatoes, heat the oven to 400 degrees. Wash 2 large heads of garlic. Cut across the top of the head just enough to expose the cloves. Place a 6-inch square of heavy-duty aluminum foil on your work surface and place the heads of garlic on the foil, cut side up. Drizzle with a little olive oil and enclose the garlic completely by bringing the foil up and over, crimping the top. Place in the oven and roast until tender, about a half an hour. When done, set aside until the garlic is cool enough to handle, then squeeze the softened garlic cloves into a small bowl. Mash until smooth and set aside. Next, purée enough roasted green chile to make 2 tablespoons.

Meanwhile, boil the potatoes in salted water until they are tender, about 15 minutes. Drain the potatoes and transfer them to a baking sheet. Place in the oven for about 10 minutes to dry the potatoes. Transfer them to a large bowl and add the milk and butter. Using an electric mixer or a potato masher, combine ingredients until smooth. Add 2 tablespoons each of the roasted garlic and the green chile purée and mix until incorporated. Season to taste. Keep the mashed potatoes hot until serving time by placing the mixing bowl over a pan of simmering water, stirring the mixture occasionally.

To prepare the sauce, sauté the onions and jalapeño over medium heat in a small stainless steel saucepan. Add the blueberries, brown sugar, vinegar, ketchup, mustard and Tabasco sauce. Cook at a low boil for 15 minutes, stirring often. Purée the sauce in a food processor or blender, then strain it. Whisk in the butter and season to taste.

Put the steaks on a hot grill and cook to your preferred doneness, about 4 to 5 minutes on each side for medium rare. Meanwhile, heat the butter in a skillet over medium-high heat and sauté the red bell pepper and red onion until just soft. Add the green beans, fava beans and corn and stir to mix. Continue to cook for about another minute. Season to taste.

When ready to serve, cover the bottom of each dinner plate with blueberry barbecue sauce and follow with a generous spoonful of mashed potatoes placed slightly off-center. Lean a steak against the potatoes and spoon a portion of the vegetable mixture across the top of the plate. Sprinkle with fresh blueberries.

MARK MILITELLO

MARK'S PLACE
MIAMI

*S*outh Florida's most celebrated chef, Mark Militello, is a native Texan who was raised in upstate New York. Intending to become a doctor, he enrolled in the pre-med program at Marquette University but realized during his first year that food and hospitality were his true calling. Trading his scalpel for a chef's knife, he switched schools and careers, earning culinary degrees from New York State University's Hotel and Culinary Program as well as Florida International University's School of Hospitality and Hotel Management.

The climate and the remarkable variety of indigenous ingredients in Florida and its surrounding waters proved catalysts for Mark's creativity. He worked for several years in hotels and restaurants there before becoming chef at Café Max, Max's Place and Maxaluna in the early eighties. During this period he developed relationships with farmers and fishermen to improve the quality and availability of local products. He also refined his own culinary vision of a cuisine influenced by Provence and the dynamic California culinary movement, accented by the sunny flavors of the Caribbean.

In 1988, he struck out on his own and opened Mark's Place in North Miami. Within a year he had received top ratings from the *Miami Herald* and *South Florida* magazine and the attention of the national food press. *Food & Wine* named Mark one of the Ten Best Chefs in America in 1990, and in 1992 Mark's Place received an award from DiRoNA as one of the Top 25 Restaurants in the Country. That same year Mark was honored as Best American Chef: Southeast by The James Beard Foundation. The GaultMillau and Zagat guidebooks call Mark's Place the best restaurant in Florida; *Condé Nast Traveler* voted it one of the Fifty Best Restaurants in the United States; and he has twice won *GQ's* Golden Dish Award.

In August of 1994, Mark opened his second restaurant, Mark's Las Olas, in Fort Lauderdale with a menu he calls "globe-trotting bistro." A third venture, Mark's in the Grove, at the Grove Isle Club and Resort, opened in the fall of 1995. He was featured recently in the Julia Child *Cooking with Master Chefs* series on PBS and is working on a cookbook about seafood.

Sour Orange and Cumin Spiced Chicken Breast with Plantain Stuffing, Two Salsas and Black Bean Sauce

Serves 4

Ingredients

4 large boneless chicken breasts, skin on

Marinade

1-3/4 cups fresh orange juice

1/3 cup balsamic vinegar

4 tablespoons extra virgin olive oil

2 tablespoons ground cumin

1 tablespoon chili powder

1 tablespoon finely chopped garlic

1 teaspoon sugar

Salt and freshly ground black pepper

Plantain Stuffing

1 ripe plantain, peeled and cut into 1/2-inch dice

1 quart water

3 tablespoons unsalted butter

1-1/2 teaspoons sugar

1-1/2 tablespoons dark rum

1/4 cup reserved plantain cooking liquid

Salt and freshly ground pepper

Black Bean Sauce

1-1/2 cups dried black beans, rinsed and soaked
   overnight in 6 cups cold water

2 tablespoons olive oil

2 tablespoons diced smoked applewood bacon,
   or substitute other smoked bacon

1/4 cup diced onion

2 tablespoons diced red bell pepper

1/2 teaspoon minced Scotch bonnet pepper
   (use caution when handling, they are
   extremely hot), or substitute 1/2 teaspoon
   Scotch bonnet prepared sauce

1 tablespoon minced garlic

1 tablespoon ground cumin

1-1/2 teaspoons chili powder

1/4 cup chopped tomato

4 cups chicken stock

1 tablespoon dry sherry

1/2 teaspoon chopped fresh thyme leaves

1/2 teaspoon chopped cilantro leaves

1/2 teaspoon balsamic vinegar

Salt and freshly ground black pepper

Roasted Corn Salsa

1/2 cup roasted corn kernels (about 1 ear)

2 tablespoons roasted, peeled, seeded and
   diced poblano chile

1 tablespoon diced red bell pepper

1 tablespoon diced red onion

2 teaspoons chopped cilantro

1 tablespoon extra virgin olive oil

1 tablespoon fresh lime juice

Salt and freshly ground pepper to taste

Avocado Salsa

1 cup diced ripe Haas avocado

1/4 cup diced red onion

2 tablespoons chopped cilantro

2 tablespoons chopped green onion

2 tablespoons extra virgin olive oil

Juice of 1 lime

1 pound calabaza (West Indian pumpkin), or
    substitute another variety of squash, peeled,
    seeded and cut into 1/2-inch dice

Combine the marinade ingredients in a large ceramic or glass bowl. Marinate the chicken breasts in this mixture, turning occasionally, for 4 to 6 hours.

Meanwhile, prepare the plantain stuffing. Place the diced plantain, water, butter and sugar in a heavy medium saucepan and bring to a boil. Reduce the heat and gently simmer for 30 to 40 minutes, or until tender.

Drain, reserving about 1/2 cup of the cooking liquid. Press the plantain through a food mill into a mixing bowl. Beat in the rum, enough plantain cooking liquid to make a thick purée, and salt and pepper to taste. Let the mixture cool to room temperature.

Next prepare the black bean sauce. Heat the olive oil in a large heavy sauce pan. Render the bacon over medium heat, but do not let it brown or crisp. Add the onion and bell pepper and cook until soft and translucent, but do not allow them to brown. Add the Scotch bonnet and garlic and cook until fragrant but not brown. Stir in the cumin and chili powder and cook for 2 minutes. Add the tomato and the chicken stock and bring to a boil. Reduce the heat to a simmer, add the beans and cook for 1 hour or until they are very tender. Stir in the sherry, thyme, cilantro and balsamic vinegar and simmer for 2 minutes. Purée the bean mixture in a blender, then force it through a large-holed strainer.

The mixture should have the consistency of a smooth, flowing sauce. If it is too thick, add a little more chicken stock. If too thin, boil it, stirring often, until it is reduced to the desired consistency. Season it with salt and pepper, and keep warm.

While the beans are cooking, prepare the salsas. Combine the ingredients for each salsa in separate bowls and toss each one gently to mix. Season to taste and set aside.

Cook the diced calabaza in 2 quarts of lightly salted simmering water for 5 minutes, or until tender. Drain and keep warm.

Preheat oven to 400 degrees. Remove the chicken breasts from the marinade. Using a long slender knife, cut a deep lengthwise pocket in the thickest part of each breast, taking care not to puncture the top or the bottom. Transfer the plantain mixture to a pastry bag fitted with a large round tip. Pipe the plantain stuffing into the pocket of each chicken breast, then pin it closed with a toothpick. If you don't have a pastry bag and tip, carefully spoon the stuffing into the pocket. Heat a small amount of olive oil in a large ovenproof nonstick sauté pan. Sear the chicken breasts over high heat for about 1 minute per side. Transfer the pan to a 400-degree oven and roast until done, about 10 minutes.

To serve, ladle about 1/2 cup of the black bean sauce onto the center of each large dinner plate. Place a chicken breast in the center. Put a spoonful of the roasted corn salsa to the left and a spoonful of the avocado salsa to the right. Sprinkle the diced calabaza on top of the sauce, between the chicken and the salsas.

BRADLEY OGDEN

LARK CREEK INN
SAN FRANCISCO BAY AREA

*B*radley Ogden feels that the single greatest influence on his cooking came from his childhood exposure to fresh American foods. Born in Michigan in the early '50s, he grew up enjoying freshly caught trout, free-range chickens and fruits and vegetables hand-picked in season. His formal training was at the Culinary Institute of America. He graduated with honors in 1977 and was chosen the student most likely to succeed, which he began doing immediately. He was hired as sous-chef at the American Restaurant in Kansas City and within six months was promoted to executive chef. In 1983, Bradley moved to San Francisco to become executive chef at the newly opened Campton Place Hotel. Under his direction, the hotel's restaurant earned a reputation for serving outstanding and innovative American cuisine. He left Campton Place in 1989 to open The Lark Creek Inn in nearby Larkspur with Michael Dellar as his partner. Another Ogden-Dellar project, One Market, opened in San Francisco in 1993, showcasing all-American fare in a cosmopolitan environment.

The Lark Creek Café in Walnut Creek debuted in 1995 with a homey atmosphere and farm-fresh favorites.

Bradley was named Best American Chef: California by The James Beard Foundation in 1993. He has been inducted into the Who's Who of American Cooking by *Cook's* magazine and awarded the Golden Plate Award by the American Academy of Achievement. He has represented the United States at events in Europe and Asia and has been frequently featured in such publications as *Food & Wine, Cook's, Wine Spectator, Gourmet, Bon Appétit, Metropolitan Home* and *Life*. His television credits include *The Today Show, Good Morning America* and the PBS series *Great Chefs of the West.*

With the assistance of his wife Jody, Bradley published his cookbook *Bradley Ogden's Breakfast, Lunch & Dinner* (Random House, 1991), which won a prestigious Julia Child Cookbook Award.

OAK GRILLED SALMON
WITH LENTIL SALAD, WARM DUNGENESS CRAB
AND SMOKED BACON DRESSING

Serves 4

Bradley's culinary motto: "Keep it simple; use the freshest ingredients available and put them together in such a way that the flavors, colors and textures combine to bring out the best in each dish." His Oak Grilled Salmon with Lentil Salad, Warm Dungeness Crab and Smoked Bacon Dressing fills those requirements perfectly.

INGREDIENTS

4 5-to 6-ounce salmon filets, approximately
     3/4 inch thick

1/2 teaspoon chopped fresh thyme

2 cloves garlic, peeled and cut into slivers

1/2 teaspoon grated lemon zest

1 teaspoon kosher salt

1/2 teaspoon freshly ground black pepper

3 tablespoons olive oil

LENTIL SALAD

1 cup dried lentils, ideally the small green variety
     which can be purchased at specialty food stores

3 tablespoons olive oil

2 teaspoons minced garlic

1/3 cup minced onion

1/4 cup diced celery

1/3 cup diced carrots

3 cups ham hock and tomato broth (recipe follows),
     or substitute chicken stock

3/4 teaspoon kosher salt

2 teaspoons red wine vinegar

2 tablespoons balsamic vinegar

1/4 teaspoon freshly ground black pepper

HAM HOCK AND TOMATO BROTH

     (yields approximately 1 quart)

2 smoked ham hocks

1 leek, white part only, thoroughly cleaned

1 medium yellow onion, washed and
     cut into quarters

2 medium carrots, peeled

2 celery stalks, washed

2 heads garlic, washed and cut in half

2 serrano chile peppers, chopped

2 tablespoons canned ancho chile paste, available at
     Latin American markets or specialty food shops
     (if difficult to find this can be omitted)

5 large tomatoes, cut in half

8 to 10 large sprigs of fresh thyme

1 bay leaf

2 cups chicken stock

6 cups water

DUNGENESS CRAB AND SMOKED BACON DRESSING

2 slices smoked bacon, minced

1 clove garlic, minced

1 teaspoon Dijon mustard

2 teaspoons red wine vinegar

1 tablespoon plus 1 teaspoon balsamic vinegar

1/3 cup olive oil

2 tablespoons coarsely chopped Italian parsley

2 tablespoons chopped chives

2 tablespoons finely diced tomato

Kosher salt and freshly ground black pepper to taste

1/3 cup fresh Dungeness crab meat

1-1/2 cups small arugula leaves, washed and dried

On a clean work surface, crush the thyme, garlic, lemon zest, salt and pepper together with the flat of a knife blade. Rub the salmon with the herb mixture and 1/4 cup olive oil. Cover and marinate for several hours or overnight.

If you are making the ham hock and tomato broth, you will need to start at least 5 hours before you plan to serve. Preheat the oven to 350 degrees. Combine all of the ingredients in a large roasting pan and place in the oven for 3 hours. Remove pan from oven and strain the broth through a fine sieve. Cool immediately in an ice bath and refrigerate or freeze until needed.

To prepare the lentil salad, rinse the lentils in cold water and drain. In a large saucepan, heat the olive oil over medium heat. Add the minced vegetables and sauté, stirring occasionally, for 5 minutes. Add the lentils, the ham hock and tomato broth and the salt. Bring to a simmer. Lower the heat, cover and simmer until the lentils are tender, about half an hour to 45 minutes depending on the lentils. Add more broth during the cooking if necessary. Drain the cooked lentils and add the red wine vinegar, balsamic vinegar and pepper. Adjust seasoning and keep lentils warm until ready to serve.

To prepare the dressing, place the minced bacon in a small pan over low heat and cook until the fat has rendered and the bacon is light brown and crispy. Remove the bacon to drain on paper towels, then discard all but a teaspoon of the fat in the pan. Set aside. In a small bowl, whisk together the mustard, red wine vinegar, balsamic vinegar and olive oil. Set aside.

When ready to serve, grill the salmon filets over hot coals until medium rare, about 4 minutes per side.

While the salmon is grilling, sauté the minced garlic in the remaining bacon fat for a minute. Add the vinegar and oil mixture, the bacon, the chopped tomato and herbs and stir. Add the crab meat at the last minute.

Toss the arugula with a touch of balsamic vinegar and extra virgin olive oil to lightly coat the leaves. Season with salt and pepper.

To serve, spoon the warm lentil salad on a serving platter or on four individual dinner plates. In the center, arrange the arugula loosely and top with the grilled salmon. Generously spoon the dressing over the salmon.

LOUIS OSTEEN

LOUIS'S CHARLESTON GRILL
CHARLESTON, SOUTH CAROLINA

*L*ouis Osteen is a native of South Carolina, the son and grandson of cinema owners. After graduating from the University of South Carolina with a degree in business, he joined the family company in Atlanta. In 1975, he left the traditional livelihood of his forebears to pursue his passion for cooking. He apprenticed in the kitchens of various Atlanta restaurants, most notably with François Delcros, at that time the most celebrated chef in the area. After learning every position from prep cook to executive chef, he began the search for his own place.

Louis and his wife Marlene moved to Pawleys Island, South Carolina in 1980, and opened the Pawleys Island Inn. It was here in the coastal marshes of South Carolina that Louis began to explore Lowcountry cooking. He discovered a rich heritage of recipes featuring an abundance of local seafood, grains and game, and he soon became a leader of the movement toward indigenous American food that was just beginning to sweep the country. The philosophy of Louis and his colleagues is to showcase traditional regional ingredients and preparations at the highest level of quality. At the same time the American consumer began to prefer this fresh approach rather than pale imitations of "continental cuisine." With the originality of his recipes, the honesty of his technique and his overwhelming enthusiasm for his locale, Louis gained the attention and admiration of the regional and national press.

In 1989 Louis's desire to reach a larger clientele led to Charleston and the opening of Louis's Charleston Grill. That first year the Grill was named one of the country's Top 25 New Restaurants by *Esquire* magazine. He has also received the Ivy Award, been inducted into the Fine Dining Hall of Fame, won the DiRoNA, and been twice recognized by The James Beard Foundation for his superb Lowcountry cooking. In 1995, Louis's was featured in articles in *Bon Appétit*, *GQ*, *Southern Living* and *Esquire*. An ardent promoter of his profession and his community, Louis serves on the boards of the New England Culinary Institute and DiRoNA and is a founder and co-chair of the Charleston Taste of the Nation event.

Pork Porterhouse
with Braised Fall Cabbage

Serves 4

Ingredients

4 center-cut pork chops, closely trimmed, weighing
    about 12 ounces each

4 cloves garlic, minced

16 juniper berries, crushed

12 fresh sage leaves, finely minced

2 teaspoons kosher salt

1/2 teaspoon freshly ground black pepper

4 tablespoons peanut oil

2 cups chicken stock

Small sprig of thyme

Braised Cabbage

1 head of green cabbage, about 2 pounds

6 tablespoons butter

1 cup chicken stock

Salt and freshly ground black pepper

Sprinkle the pork chops with the garlic, juniper
berries, sage and salt. Cover loosely with plastic
wrap and refrigerate for at least 3 hours,
or overnight.

About 30 minutes before you want to serve, trim the
cabbage of any tough outer leaves. Quarter the

cabbage, cut out and discard the dense central core,
then slice the cabbage into fine shreds. In a large
heavy sauté pan, melt the butter over medium-high
heat. When the butter foams, add the cabbage and
sauté until it begins to color slightly. Add the
chicken stock and salt and pepper to taste. Reduce
the heat and simmer for 15 minutes. The cabbage
should be tender but still a bit crisp.

While the cabbage is simmering, prepare the pork
chops. Lightly scrape the herbs and spices from the
pork chops, then pat the chops dry with a paper
towel. Heat a heavy skillet over medium heat and
add the peanut oil. When the oil is hot but not
smoking, add the pork chops. Do not crowd the
chops—cook them in two pans or in two batches if
necessary. Adjust the heat to medium. It is important
that the chops cook gently so they will not toughen.
Turn the chops only once and remove them from
the pan when they are cooked to medium doneness,
internal temperature about 140 degrees. Always try
to cook the chops at the last minute so that it is not
necessary to hold them in a warming oven, where
they could dry out.

Remove the chops to a heated serving platter, cover with foil and hold in a warm spot. Pour the fat from the pan. Add the chicken stock and the sprig of thyme and reduce by half over high heat. Strain the light sauce into a warm bowl. Place the braised cabbage in a warm dish and serve everything family style.

Chef's Note: "Traditionally in the South, streak o' lean was the cooking fat of choice. It is the BMW of fatback because of its high proportion of lean meat. This is how you would prepare the cabbage using streak o' lean: Cut a 1/4-pound piece of lean salt pork into 1/4-inch slices. Place them in a cold 10-inch black cast iron skillet. Cook over very low heat for about 20 minutes to render the fat. Turn the heat up to medium and continue to cook until the meat is crisp. Remove the meat with a slotted spoon, drain it on a paper towel and reserve. Raise the heat to medium high and continue with the recipe, omitting the butter. When the cabbage is ready to serve, stir in the reserved crisped streak o' lean."

CHARLES PALMER

AUREOLE
NEW YORK

Charles Palmer began his career while still a high school student in Smyrna, New York, in the heart of upstate farm country. He went on to hone his skills at the Culinary Institute of America, then joined the team that successfully reopened Manhattan's La Côte Basque. Three years later, Charles left to become chef at the Waccabuc Country Club in Westchester County, New York. He saw this move as a perfect opportunity to run his own kitchen and explore his interest in American food. In 1983, Charles was hired as executive chef at The River Café in Brooklyn. While there he set up a network of small farmers who provided the restaurant with 70 per cent of its produce as well as the majority of its other staples. Bryan Miller of *The New York Times* increased the restaurant's stars from one to three.

In November 1988, at the age of 28, Charles opened his first restaurant, Aureole, in an elegant New York City brownstone. The dining space is resplendent with quilted tapestry ceilings, dramatically lit sandstone reliefs and colossal arrangements of fresh flowers—a perfect setting for his refined interpretation of American cuisine. Aureole was awarded three stars by *The New York Times* and four stars by *Forbes;* it has been named one of America's Top 25 Restaurants by *Food & Wine* and DiRoNA and has received outstanding reviews in *Gourmet* and *Condé Nast Traveler.* The Zagat survey of New York restaurants ranked it number one in the category of American cuisine. He has appeared with Julia Child on her PBS series, *Cooking with Master Chefs,* as well as the *Today Show, Good Morning America* and the Television Food Network.

Charles has enjoyed great success in his subsequent ventures. He founded the Chef Cuisiniers Club in 1990 as a place where restaurant people could meet after work. In 1994, the CC Club was rethought, remodeled and rechristened as Alva, a spot that critic Gael Greene calls a "house of amiable spirits and outsize rations." His most recent restaurant is the handsome Lenox Room on the Upper East Side. He is also a partner in the Egg Farm Dairy, an upstate creamery producing a wide range of artisanal cheeses, and Stonekelly, a flower business that creates the arrangements for his restaurants. In 1996 Random House will publish his first cookbook.

SEARED LAMB MEDALLIONS
WITH LENTIL CAKES AND FRESH THYME

Serves 4

The richness of lamb, earthiness of lentils, sweetness of carrots and pungency of thyme—all pair beautifully with Pinot Noir.

INGREDIENTS

8 3-ounce lamb medallions, cut about 3/4 inch thick

Coarse salt and freshly ground pepper

1 tablespoon vegetable oil

SAUCE

1 medium onion

1 medium carrot

1 small stalk celery

3/4 pound lamb bones and scraps

1/2 cup white wine

3 cups water

1-1/2 cup veal stock or rich chicken stock

1 bouquet garni of 1 bay leaf, 5 peppercorns,
    1 teaspoon dried thyme, and a few stems of
    parsley, tied up in cheesecloth

3 sprigs of fresh thyme

LENTIL CAKES

5 tablespoons dried lentils

1-1/2 cups water

1 clove garlic, peeled

1 small bay leaf

1 small sprig fresh thyme

Kosher salt to taste

Freshly ground black pepper to taste

1/4 cup whole milk

1 tablespoon unsalted butter

1/2 cup all purpose flour

2-1/4 teaspoons baking powder

1 large egg

1 teaspoon sugar

1 tablespoon vegetable oil

8 small young carrots, peeled, with greens
    trimmed to 3/4 inch

1 teaspoon chopped Italian parsley

1 tablespoon unsalted butter

Season the lamb medallions with salt and freshly ground pepper, and set aside, refrigerated.

To prepare the sauce, preheat the oven to 400 degrees. Peel, trim and chop the onion, carrot and celery. Cut the lamb bones and scraps into pieces no larger than 2 inches. Place a roasting pan in the preheated oven for 3 minutes or until very hot. Remove the pan and add the lamb bones and chopped vegetables. Return the pan to the oven and roast the mixture, stirring occasionally, for 25 minutes or until well browned. Remove the pan from the oven and place on the stove over medium heat. Add the wine and stir to deglaze the pan. Simmer for 5 minutes. Add the water, stock, bouquet garni and thyme sprigs and bring to a boil. Lower heat and simmer for 30 minutes. Remove from heat and strain through a fine sieve into a medium saucepan, pushing on the solids to extract all of the liquid. Discard solids. Skim any fat off the top of the sauce. Place over medium-high heat and bring to a boil. Lower heat and simmer for 20 minutes or until the liquid is reduced to 1-1/2 cups. Remove from heat and set aside.

Meanwhile, prepare the lentil cakes. Wash the lentils well. Combine with the water, garlic, bay leaf and thyme in a medium saucepan over high heat. Bring to a boil. Lower heat and simmer for 20 minutes or until the lentils are tender but still holding their shape, adding more water if necessary. Remove from the heat and season to taste with salt and pepper. Set aside and allow to cool. When cool, drain well, picking out the garlic and herbs and discarding them. Set the cooled lentils aside. Combine the milk and butter in a small saucepan over medium heat. Cook for 1 minute or until just warm. Remove from heat. Sift flour and baking powder into a medium mixing bowl. In a separate small bowl, combine the egg and sugar and whisk to combine. Continuing to whisk, add the warm milk mixture, mixing until well blended. Slowly whisk the liquid into the dry ingredients, stirring to blend. Carefully fold in the lentils. Taste the batter and adjust seasoning with salt and pepper.

Using a 1-3/4-inch ring mold as a guide, shape the batter into small firm cakes. Heat the vegetable oil in a large, nonstick sauté pan over medium heat. Add the lentil cakes and fry until golden, about 4 minutes. Turn with a spatula and cook for an additional 4 minutes, or until the cakes are cooked through and golden brown. Hold in a warm oven while you prepare the carrots and the lamb medallions; the lentil cakes can also be made ahead and reheated.

Place the peeled and trimmed carrots in boiling salted water and blanch for about 3 minutes, or until cooked through but still firm. Drain and refresh under cold water.

About 5 minutes before you are ready to serve, heat the vegetable oil in a large sauté pan over medium-high heat. Add the lamb medallions and sear for 2 minutes. Turn and sear for an additional 2 minutes.

While the lamb is cooking, reheat the lentil cakes, if necessary, by placing them in a 300-degree oven for about 5 minutes. Melt the butter in a medium sauté pan over medium heat. Add the blanched carrots and the chopped parsley. Sauté for 2 minutes, or until heated through. Season with salt and pepper.

When you are ready to serve, place two lentil cakes in the center of each of four warm dinner plates. Set a lamb medallion on top of each lentil cake. Spoon sauce over the lamb and lentil cakes generously, so that some sauce flows onto the plate. Lean the carrots against the lentil cakes. Serve immediately.

WOLFGANG PUCK

SPAGO
LOS ANGELES

The man who is one of America's best known chefs is a native of Austria. It was there, inspired by his mother who was a chef in a hotel kitchen, that Wolfgang Puck began his formal training at the age of 14. His enthusiasm for his studies landed him an apprenticeship at L'Oustau de Baumanière in Provence, and later at other Michelin three-star restaurants including Hôtel de Paris in Monaco and Maxim's in Paris. Wolfgang came to the United States in 1973, and within a short time was the star attraction of Los Angeles' Ma Maison. Impressed with the wide variety of California produce and specialty food available to him, his personal style of cooking became freer, fresher, more contemporary. In 1984, he opened Spago on the Sunset Strip in partnership with his wife, designer Barbara Lazaroff.

With its trend-setting open kitchen, artsy interior and innovative pizzas, Spago became a temple of California Cuisine. Among the many awards the restaurant has won over the years is the prestigious Outstanding Restaurant Award from The James Beard Foundation in 1994. In a second project, Chinois on Main, which opened in Santa Monica in 1983, Barbara created a wildly exotic decor to complement the imaginative Eurasian flavors of Wolfgang's menu. At Granita in Malibu, the ambience shimmers with the colors of the Mediterranean, and the menu features Wolfgang's interpretation of the dishes of Provence and Italy. Outside southern California, Wolfgang has opened Postrio in the Prescott Hotel just off San Francisco's Union Square. In December of 1992, Spago Las Vegas debuted at Caesar's Palace, with a menu that offers popular specialties from Spago, Chinois on Main, Granita and Postrio. Spago Mexico was established in Mexico City in 1994, with rave reviews from the outset.

The Puck/Lazaroff team has recently branched out into the casual dining arena, introducing their Wolfgang Puck Café concept into department stores, shopping districts and even the University of Southern California. Other ventures include the Wolfgang Puck Food Company, which makes a line of premium frozen pizzas and pastas, an instructional cooking video, *Spago Cooking with Wolfgang Puck*, and a cookbook, *Adventures in the Kitchen with Wolfgang Puck* (Random House, 1991).

ROASTED SALMON
WITH GINGER CRUST AND POTATO PURÉE

Serves 4

Wolfgang's recipe is ideal for entertaining a crowd since the salmon can be readied earlier in the day, then roasted at the last minute.

INGREDIENTS

4 center-cut salmon filets, 6 to 7 ounces each

Salt

2 tablespoons unsalted butter, melted

1-1/2 tablespoons crushed black peppercorns

1-1/2 tablespoons finely chopped fresh
     peeled ginger

RED WINE SAUCE

6 tablespoons unsalted butter

3 large shallots, finely chopped

2 garlic cloves, finely chopped

1 plum tomato, peeled, seeded and chopped

2 cups dry red wine

1 tablespoon balsamic vinegar

1 cup chicken stock

Salt and freshly ground pepper

POTATO PURÉE

4 ounces russet potatoes (1 or 2 small potatoes),
     peeled and cut into 1-inch cubes

1 teaspoon salt

1/2 cup heavy cream

2 tablespoons unsalted butter

Freshly ground white pepper

2 tablespoons olive oil

Season the salmon lightly with salt, brush the top with a little of the melted butter and immediately sprinkle with the crushed pepper and chopped ginger. Drizzle the remaining butter over the top. If you wait too long, the butter will harden and the ginger and pepper will not stick. Refrigerate, covered, until needed.

To prepare the sauce, in a small sauté pan, melt 2 tablespoons butter until foamy. Add the shallots and garlic and sauté over medium heat until the shallots are translucent, 2 to 3 minutes. Stir in the tomato and cook for 1 or 2 minutes longer. Pour in the wine and vinegar, turn up the heat a little and reduce until 1/2 cup liquid remains. Pour in the chicken stock and reduce by half. Strain the sauce into a clean pan. Finish the sauce by whisking in the remaining 4 tablespoons of butter and season to taste with salt and pepper. Keep warm.

While the sauce is reducing, prepare the potato purée. Place the cubed potato in a medium saucepan and cover with cold water. Season with salt and cook until soft, 15 to 20 minutes. Pour off the water and return the pan to the stove. Add the cream and simmer over medium heat, stirring occasionally to prevent sticking, until the mixture has thickened and most of the cream is absorbed, about 10 minutes. Remove from the heat, stir in the butter and season with salt and pepper to taste. Purée the potato with a food mill or an electric mixer, then return to the pan. Keep the purée warm over a pan of simmering water until you are ready to serve.

Preheat the oven to 500 degrees. Ten minutes before serving, brush a baking sheet with olive oil and arrange the salmon on it in one layer. Roast until medium, about 10 minutes. The salmon should be cooked on the outside but still moist and slightly underdone inside.

Divide the sauce among four warm dinner plates. Spoon equal amounts of the potato purée into the center of each plate and place a salmon filet on top. Serve immediately.

JIMMY SCHMIDT

THE RATTLESNAKE CLUB
DETROIT

*A*native Midwesterner, Jimmy Schmidt was studying electrical engineering at the University of Illinois when he was suddenly taken with a desire to travel in France. While enrolled in language courses in Avignon, he decided to enrich his cultural studies with a course in French cooking. There he learned the basic techniques, but most importantly he met his mentor, Madeleine Kamman. When she returned to Boston to open her cooking school and restaurant, he followed. Two years later, it was she who introduced the young cook to the owner of the London Chop House in Detroit. Jimmy started in the kitchen as a cook, skyrocketed through the ranks and, a few months later, at age 22, was made executive chef. While there he was named to *Cook's* First Annual Who's Who of Cooking in America and included in the *Food & Wine* Honor Roll of American Chefs.

In 1985, Jimmy opened The Rattlesnake Club in Denver, which was named the Top New Restaurant in America by *Cook's* and *Restaurants & Institutions* and one of the Best New Restaurants by *Esquire*. When he returned to Detroit in 1988 to launch The Rattlesnake Club there, the accolades continued to roll in, including an Ivy Award, The Fine Dining Hall of Fame, DiRoNA awards and the Golden Plate Award. Jimmy was named Best American Chef: Midwest by The James Beard Foundation in 1993.

His restaurant group now owns several restaurants in the Detroit area—Stelline, Chianti Villa Italia and Chianti Villa Lago—and has returned to Denver with the Rattlesnake Grill, which opened in 1994.

Jimmy is the author of *Cooking for All Seasons* (MacMillan, 1991) and *Jimmy Schmidt's Cooking Class* (Detroit Free Press, 1994). He also writes a weekly column for the *Detroit Free Press*. He has co-authored a book with Alice Waters and Larry Forgione, *Heart Healthy Cooking for All Seasons*, which was published in February of 1996.

Jimmy is the head of Chefs' Collaborative 2000, a network of culinary leaders dedicated to increasing public awareness of healthier, more ecologically sound food choices. The group is currently producing a video for distribution to school children on the importance of local and seasonal food.

Breast of Duck
with Pinot Noir, Pears and Rosemary

Serves 4

In Jimmy's masterful recipe, he has balanced the sumptuous flavors of duck and foie gras with the punch of rosemary and black pepper, then added layers of sweetness with pears, parsnips and shallots to reflect the fruit in the wine. If foie gras is too rich for your blood, the recipe remains superb without it.

INGREDIENTS

4 boneless duck breasts, skinned and trimmed of
    all fat, about 6 or 7 ounces each
4 slices of foie gras, about 1/2 inch thick
4 small Bosc pears, cores removed with a small
    melon baller through the base, leaving the
    stems intact
2 cups medium shallots, peeled
1/4 cup olive oil
Sea salt
Freshly ground black pepper
1/4 cup fresh rosemary leaves
2 cups Pinot Noir
2 cups chicken stock

MASHED PARSNIPS

1 small baking potato, peeled and cut into
    1-inch chunks

3 large parsnips, peeled and cut into 1-inch chunks
2 tablespoons of rosemary oil (this will be left from
    frying the rosemary above)
Sea salt
Freshly ground black pepper

Salt and pepper the duck breasts and set aside, refrigerated, with the foie gras.

Preheat the oven to 400 degrees. Place the pears upright in an ovenproof dish. In a small bowl, toss together the shallots and 1 tablespoon of the olive oil, then season with salt and pepper. Scatter the shallots around the pears in the dish. Pour 1 cup of the Pinot Noir over the pears and cook in the oven until very tender, about an hour. Remove the dish from the oven and allow to cool to room temperature.

While the pears and shallots are roasting, heat the remaining oil in a small saucepan. Add the rosemary leaves and cook until crisp, about 3 minutes. Remove the rosemary leaves and drain on paper towels. Save the infused oil for the mashed parsnips.

To prepare the mashed parsnips, put the potato and parsnips in a large pot of cold water. Bring to a simmer over medium heat and cook until very tender, about 20 minutes. Turn off the heat and allow to sit for another 3 minutes. Drain the potato and parsnips in a colander. Transfer to a food processor and purée with rosemary oil until smooth. If the consistency is too thick or too lumpy, add a little cream or milk to smooth it out. Season with salt and a generous amount of freshly ground black pepper and keep warm over a pan of simmering water until you are ready to serve.

In a large saucepan, combine the remaining wine and the stock and bring to a simmer over medium high heat. Cook until it is reduced enough to coat the back of a spoon, about 15 minutes. Salt and pepper to taste. Add the roasted shallots and keep warm.

Preheat a grill or broiler. Sear the duck breasts, skin side toward the heat source, for 4 to 5 minutes.

Turn over and cook until medium rare, about 3 or 4 more minutes, depending on the thickness of the breasts. While the duck breast is cooking, heat a medium nonstick sauté pan over high heat. Season the slices of foie gras with salt and a generous amount of black pepper. Quickly sear the foie gras on one side until browned, about 2 minutes. Turn and cook on the other side for another minute. Remove to a paper towel to drain. Keep ingredients warm while you immediately start assembling the plates.

Spoon a large dollop of mashed parsnips onto the upper third of each of four dinner plates. Position one roasted pear upright next to the mashed parsnips. Cut each duck breast into 4 or 5 slices lengthwise and fan them across the plate, slightly overlapping the parsnips. Lay the foie gras next to the sliced duck breast. Spoon the shallots over the pear and foie gras, then drizzle the remaining sauce over the duck and around the plate. Sprinkle the fried rosemary leaves on top of the sauce. Garnish with a sprig of fresh rosemary.

CORY SCHREIBER

WILDWOOD
PORTLAND, OREGON

Cory Schreiber, chef/owner of Wildwood, comes from a family with a long and illustrious role in Oregon's culinary history. The Schreibers have been involved in the Northwest shellfish business since the mid-1800s, buying and selling oyster seed and oysters up and down the West Coast. Their seafood venture branched out into the restaurant business early on; by the time Cory was born in 1961, Dan & Louis' Oyster Bar had been a Portland institution for generations. At 11 Cory started his career by helping out behind the scenes.

Appreciating the solid foundation the family business had given him, Cory set out to expand his horizons by studying with restaurateurs and chefs around the United States. He worked with Lydia Shire at Seasons Restaurant in Boston, Gordon Sinclair at Gordon's in Chicago and Bradley Ogden at the Lark Creek Inn near San Francisco. He was then hired as executive chef at the Cypress Club in San Francisco, where he received great reviews in the national press.

In 1994 Cory returned to Portland to open Wildwood, which won notice from *Esquire* as one of the year's Best New Restaurants. In 1995 Wildwood was featured in articles in *The New York Times*, *USA Today* and *Esquire*. The restaurant's decor is contemporary Northwest, with slate and wood floors, Douglas fir tables and a ceramic and glass mural that is a tribute to both the regional bounty and to Portland's legendary son, James Beard. An open kitchen with wood ovens brings warmth, literally and figuratively, into the dining room. The changing menu is designed to highlight seasonal ingredients from nearby farms and forests. While there is an understandable emphasis on seafood, the kitchen also does an excellent job with local lamb, poultry and game.

Shortly after opening Wildwood in 1994, Cory organized the Autumn Food and Wine Festival, which has become an annual harvest event. By day there are cooking demonstrations, live music and outdoor booths manned by specialty purveyors and Oregon wineries. In the evening the restaurant hosts a collaborative dinner with Portland's top chefs—all proceeds go to charity.

This fifth generation Portlander is home.

WILD MUSHROOM TOASTS
WITH ROASTED GARLIC, CARAMELIZED ONIONS
AND GOAT CHEESE

Serves 4

This recipe is an excellent choice for a first course or light luncheon dish. The toasts can also be made smaller and served as hors d'oeuvres. An added attraction is that every step up to the final assembly can be done the day before.

INGREDIENTS

4 large heads of garlic

Olive oil

Salt and freshly ground black pepper

1 pound wild mushrooms, such as morels or
    chanterelles (cultivated mushrooms may
    be substituted)

2 medium white onions

2 tablespoons olive oil

2 tablespoons balsamic vinegar

1 tablespoon Dijon mustard

1 teaspoon chopped fresh thyme leaves

8 slices hard-crusted bread, cut 3/4 inch thick and
    3 to 4 inches long (a baguette cut on the bias
    works perfectly)

1/4 pound mesclun or mix of baby lettuces

4 ounces fresh goat cheese, crumbled

Olive oil

RED WINE VINAIGRETTE

2 tablespoons olive oil

1 teaspoon red wine vinegar

1/2 teaspoon Dijon mustard

Salt and pepper

Preheat oven to 350 degrees. Cut the top off the heads of garlic, exposing the cloves but keeping the heads intact. Place the garlic in a small ovenproof dish, drizzle with a little olive oil, and season with salt and pepper. Cover tightly with aluminum foil, place on a middle rack in the oven and bake until the cloves are soft, about an hour. Remove from the oven and cool.

Next, clean the wild mushrooms and spread them on a cookie sheet in one layer. Season with salt and pepper. Place in the oven on a rack above the garlic and bake until almost dry. The mushrooms will give off their moisture initially and then begin to dry, concentrating their flavors. This will take 20 to 30 minutes. When cooked, remove from the oven and set aside to cool.

While the garlic and mushrooms are in the oven, prepare the caramelized onions. Peel the onions and slice them thinly. Pour 2 tablespoons of olive oil into a medium sauté pan and place over medium-low heat. Add the onions and season with salt and pepper. Cook the onions slowly, stirring them frequently. They will slowly caramelize over a period of 30 to 40 minutes, turning a rich golden brown. Add the balsamic vinegar and stir, deglazing the pan. Cook for 5 minutes longer while the caramelized onions absorb the flavor of the vinegar. Adjust seasoning and set aside to cool.

Squeeze the softened garlic pulp from the cloves into a small bowl. Stir in the Dijon mustard and chopped thyme to make a smooth spread. Season with salt and pepper and reserve.

Wash the greens and dry well. Make the vinaigrette by whisking the ingredients together.

Just before you are ready to serve, brush the sliced bread with olive oil and place on a cookie sheet. Toast in a 350-degree oven for 5 minutes, or until crusty on the outside but still soft in the center. Remove from oven. Spread each piece of bread with the roasted garlic mixture and a thick layer of caramelized onions, then top with a generous portion of wild mushrooms. Return the toasts to the oven for another 5 minutes to allow the topping to warm through. Remove the toasts from the oven and place 1/2 ounce of crumbled goat cheese on top of each one. Return them to the oven to melt the cheese, approximately 4 or 5 minutes longer.

To serve, place a mushroom toast in the center of each luncheon plate, then lean a second piece against it at an angle. Toss the greens lightly with the vinaigrette and pile loosely on top of the toasts.

JOACHIM SPLICHAL

PATINA
LOS ANGELES

*J*oachim Splichal was born and raised in Spaichingen, Germany, where he worked in his family's inn and butcher shop. He gained his basic training as an apprentice in kitchens in The Netherlands, Canada, Switzerland and Sweden, but he really began to flourish when he arrived on the French Riviera. He worked alongside the highly inventive Jacques Maximin at La Bonne Auberge, then followed him to the Hôtel Négresco in Nice. After four years there as sous-chef, he moved to L'Oasis, a Michelin three-star restaurant in La Napoule, where he became a protégé of Louis Outhier. It was Outhier who brought the young Joachim to Los Angeles in 1981 to become chef at the Regency Club.

In Los Angeles, Joachim's work immediately attracted attention as some of the most exciting and imaginative of the California-French culinary movement. He left the Regency to head the kitchen at the Seventh Street Bistro, then wowed diners with his striking creations at Max au Triangle in Beverly Hills. In partnership with his wife Christine, Joachim established Patina in 1989. With its gracious and informed service and the compelling combination of whimsy and perfection coming from the kitchen, Patina is considered by many to be America's best restaurant. Joachim was named Best American Chef: California by The James Beard Foundation in 1991 and has twice been nominated for Outstanding Chef, in 1991 and 1994. In 1995 he was voted into the Foundation's Who's Who of Food & Beverages and also received an Ivy Award.

The Splichals have created a small culinary empire with the addition of Pinot Bistro, Patinette, Cafe Pinot, Pinot Hollywood and The Martini Bar, and Pinot Blanc. Pinot Bistro, which opened in 1992, has bistro fare so outstanding it was named Best New Restaurant of the Year by *Esquire*. Patinette, a café at the Museum of Contemporary Art and Cafe Pinot, a contemporary brasserie, are located in downtown Los Angeles. Pinot Blanc, in the Napa Valley wine country, and Pinot Hollywood and The Martini Bar are their most recent ventures. Joachim's first cookbook, *Patina Cookbook: Spuds, Truffles and Wild Gnocchi* (Collins, 1995), offers a day-in-the-life view of a top restaurant kitchen, with documentary-style photography and a running text, as well as recipes for his signature dishes.

REALLY SLOWLY ROASTED VEAL SHANK WITH BABY VEGETABLES AND CHANTERELLES

Serves 4

This rich, full-flavored family dish satisfies the soul as well as the appetite.

INGREDIENTS

2 teaspoons extra virgin olive oil

1 4- to 5-pound veal shank

Salt and freshly ground pepper

1 medium carrot, coarsely chopped

2 stalks celery, coarsely chopped

1/2 medium yellow onion, coarsely chopped

2 cloves garlic, coarsely chopped

1 sprig fresh thyme

4 plum tomatoes, coarsely chopped

1/4 cup dry white wine

2 cups chicken stock

BABY VEGETABLES

1/4 pound baby carrots, peeled, tops trimmed to 1/4 inch

1/4 pound baby turnips, trimmed and washed

1/4 pound tiny haricots verts

1/4 pound thin asparagus, trimmed, with bottom inch of stalk peeled

1/2 pound waxy potatoes, such as Yukon Gold or White Rose, peeled and cut into quarters

1/4 pound cherry tomatoes

1 cup fresh peas (about 1/2 pound in the pod)

1/4 pound fresh spinach leaves, stems removed

1/4 pound fresh fava beans, blanched for 2 minutes in boiling water and shells removed

CHANTERELLES

1 tablespoon unsalted butter

1 small shallot, finely chopped

4 ounces fresh chanterelles, or other wild or cultivated mushroom of your choice, wiped clean

Salt and freshly ground white pepper

1 ounce unsalted butter, at room temperature, cut into 2 pieces

2 tablespoons finely chopped chives

In a large ovenproof sauté pan, heat the oil over high heat. Using heavy kitchen tongs and a carving fork to steady the meat, sear the veal shank evenly for about 6 to 7 minutes, or until all sides are golden brown. Season the shank with salt and pepper to taste, and remove it to a large ovenproof braising pan or oval Dutch oven. Meanwhile, preheat the oven to 325 degrees. Add the carrot, celery and onion to the sauté pan and reduce the heat to medium. Cook the vegetables, stirring occasionally to prevent them from burning, for 8 to 10 minutes or until golden. Add the garlic, thyme and tomatoes and cook, stirring, until the garlic releases its aroma, about 1 minute. Add the wine to the pan and deglaze, stirring and scraping the bottom and sides so that all the flavorful bits are released into the liquid. Add the stock, stir to mix well, and pour the mixture over the veal shank in the braising pan. Cover the pan and cook in the oven for 2-1/2 to 3 hours, basting the shank with the liquid in the pan every 10 to 15 minutes. Turn the shank over every 30 minutes. When done, remove the shank to an ovenproof platter, cover and set aside. Strain the braising juices into a large saucepan and discard the solids. Over high heat, reduce the braising liquid by about three quarters, skimming off the fat and impurities. When reduced, cover and set aside.

To prepare the vegetables, have a large bowl of ice water ready. In a large saucepan, bring a generous amount of water to a boil. Blanch each type of vegetable separately by plunging it into the boiling water and cooking for 1 to 4 minutes depending on the size, or until cooked al dente. Using a skimmer, remove the vegetables and immediately plunge them into the ice water for 1 minute to stop the cooking and set the color. Drain the vegetables on a clean towel. Proceed until all the vegetables have been blanched, chilled and drained. (You may need to add more ice to the water as you go.)

To prepare the chanterelles, melt the butter in a small sauté pan over medium heat. Add the shallots and cook, stirring occasionally, for 3 to 4 minutes, or until softened. Add the chanterelles and cook for 4 to 5 minutes, stirring occasionally, until tender. Season to taste with salt and pepper.

When you are ready to serve, reheat the veal shank, if necessary, still covered with foil, in a 350-degree oven for 10 to 15 minutes, or until heated through. Return the braising liquid to a simmer and swirl in the butter, a piece at a time, until it is just absorbed and the sauce becomes glossy. Add the vegetables and chanterelles to the saucepan and turn them gently until they are heated through and coated with the sauce.

Place the veal shank in the center of a large heated oval serving platter. Remove the vegetables from the sauce with a slotted spoon and arrange them loosely in an attractive mix around the shank. Drizzle the remaining sauce over the shank and sprinkle the chives over all. Serve family-style.

STEPHANIE PEARL KIMMEL

KING ESTATE
EUGENE, OREGON

 native of Texas, Stephanie grew up living and traveling around the world. Her father was an Air Force pilot with assignments in Japan, Europe and North Africa, as well as in many regions of the United States. Her parents, both enthusiastic cooks and cultural explorers, engendered in her a love and appreciation for diverse culinary traditions.

Stephanie's formal education was in English Literature and French Cultural History, with degrees from the University of Oregon and the Sorbonne. As a graduate student in Comparative Literature, she took her first restaurant job to help pay for educational expenses, and it was there she discovered her real passion. Her lifelong interest in cooking evolved into her métier. In 1972, she opened the Excelsior Café in Eugene, Oregon, pioneering a Northwest culinary movement with her use of seasonal menus that celebrated the bounty of the region. The restaurant was also the first in Oregon to feature the wines of the young Oregon wine industry. During her tenure there as chef/owner, the Excelsior Café was featured in *Cook's, Food & Wine, Gourmet, Travel and Leisure, Bon Appétit, Sunset, Nation's Restaurant News.*

After selling the restaurant in the spring of 1993, Stephanie took an extended trip to France to explore regional markets and vineyards. In September of 1993, she joined the team at King Estate as Culinary Director. Her current responsibilities include preparing meals for guests; research, recipe testing, and writing about food and wine; and supervising a full-scale hospitality program. She also works with the gardeners on planning and planting the organic vegetable and flower garden, berry patches and orchards. The development of a line of food products from the property is in progress. Recently she participated in the realization of a 13-part cooking series, *New American Cuisine*, in conjunction with Oregon Public Broadcasting. *New American Cuisine* will be seen on PBS stations nationally.

In 1995, the *King Estate Pinot Gris Cookbook*, which Stephanie compiled and edited, was published, receiving highly favorable reviews in a number of food and wine publications.

Oregon Blue Cheese Gougères

Makes about 24 3-inch puffs

These moist cheese puffs are the traditional harvest snack for the grape growers and winemakers of Burgundy. I created this version with the blue cheese from the Rogue River Valley Creamery to complement Oregon's wonderful Pinot Noir.

10 tablespoons unsalted butter

3/4 teaspoon salt

2 cups unbleached flour, sifted

5 large eggs

1 cup Oregon blue cheese, crumbled
    (or substitute another blue-veined cheese)

Freshly ground black pepper

1 egg, beaten

Preheat oven to 375 degrees. Combine 1-1/2 cups of water, butter and salt in a saucepan and bring to a boil. Remove from the heat immediately and add all of the flour at once, stirring vigorously with a wooden spoon. When the flour is incorporated, return the pan to the heat for several minutes, stirring constantly until the mixture starts to dry out and pull away from the edge of the pan. Away from the heat, add the eggs one at a time, mixing each one until well blended. The dough should be soft and shiny. Add the blue cheese. Season with black pepper and more salt if needed.

Butter a baking sheet. Using either a soup spoon or a pastry bag with a large plain tip, make mounds about 2 inches in diameter. Using a pastry brush, paint tops with a glaze of the beaten egg. Bake for about 35 minutes, or until puffed and golden brown.

The puffs are at their best when served warm from the oven, but are also delicious at room temperature. They can be made ahead and frozen, then popped in the oven to reheat just before serving.

Roasted Beef Tenderloin with Morel Sauce and Straw Potatoes with Leeks

Serves 4

This is a lovely combination of flavors for an elegant early spring dinner. Start with a warm asparagus salad dressed with hazelnut vinaigrette and follow with a bright lemon custard tart for dessert.

Ingredients

1-1/2 pound piece of beef tenderloin, trimmed
    of all fat and membrane

Salt and freshly ground pepper

6 ounces fresh morel mushrooms or
    1-1/2 ounces dried morels

3 tablespoon unsalted butter

1 tablespoon finely chopped shallot

1/2 cup Pinot Noir, plus an additional 1/4 cup
    for deglazing roasting pan

3/4 cup heavy cream

2 tablespoons veal demi-glace, or
    substitute 1/2 cup good beef stock

1 tablespoon fresh lemon juice

1 tablespoon olive oil for sautéing

Straw Potatoes with Leeks

2 medium leeks

1 tablespoon unsalted butter

2 medium russet potatoes, about 8 ounces, peeled
    and grated (the medium shredding disc of a
    food processor makes a nice long strand)

3 tablespoons flour

Salt and freshly ground pepper

1 egg

1 tablespoon olive oil

1 tablespoon chopped chives

1 teaspoon chopped fresh tarragon

Olive oil or peanut oil for frying

Generously season the beef tenderloin with salt and pepper and set aside.

Soak fresh morels in salted warm water for 30 minutes to release any dirt or wildlife. Rinse well and drain thoroughly on paper towels. If using dried morels, place them in a bowl and cover with boiling water, leave them for 15 minutes, then drain. Save the soaking water from the dried morels, strain it through a coffee filter and reserve for the sauce reduction.

Melt 1 tablespoon of the butter in a large skillet over medium heat. Add the morels to the pan and cook until they release their juices. Add another tablespoon of butter to the pan, turn the heat to high and sauté until the liquid has disappeared, 3 to 4 minutes. Remove the morels with a slotted spoon and reserve. Place the third tablespoon of butter in the pan. When melted, add the chopped shallots and sauté over low heat for 2 to 3 minutes, until the shallots are soft and translucent. Pour in 1/2 cup Pinot Noir and reduce by half. Add the reserved morel liquid if you used dried morels, the demi-glace or beef stock, the cream and the lemon juice. Boil until it thickens enough to coat the back of a spoon. Season with salt and pepper and hold in a warm spot until just before serving. (The sauce can be prepared a day in advance. Store the sauce and morels separately and refrigerate.)

To make the straw potatoes, cut the tops off the leeks, leaving just the white and pale green portions. Trim the root end and cut the leek in half lengthwise. Turn the cut side down and slice lengthwise into slivers. Rinse the leeks very thoroughly in a colander to remove any trace of grit. Drain the leeks well. Melt the butter in a small sauté pan, add the leeks and cook them over low heat until soft. If they start to dry out or crisp up, add a little water to the pan. Set them aside to cool. Toss the grated potatoes and the cooled leeks with the flour, salt and pepper. Whisk the egg with the oil and add to the potato mixture. Stir well to combine, add chopped herbs and stir again to incorporate evenly.

Before continuing with the potatoes, preheat the oven to 400 degrees. Heat the olive oil in a large ovenproof skillet. Add the tenderloin and cook over high heat, turning until the meat is richly browned on all sides, about 4 minutes per side. Transfer the pan to the oven and roast the meat about 10 minutes, or until the internal temperature reaches 125 degrees (medium-rare). Transfer the beef to a cutting board and tent with foil. Allow the meat to rest for 5 to 6 minutes before you slice it.

While the beef is resting, bring the sauce to a simmer over medium-low heat. Deglaze the roasting pan with 1/4 cup Pinot Noir and strain it into the sauce. Whisk to blend. Stir in the morels and taste for seasoning.

In a large skillet, pour oil for frying to a depth of 3/4 inch. Heat oil until quite hot, but not smoking—you can test by dropping a bit of the batter in the pan; it will sizzle when the oil is ready. Loosely spoon the batter into the pan, about 2 tablespoonsful at a time. Don't worry if the strands jut out in an irregular fashion; it adds to the "straw" character. When the cakes are golden on the bottom, turn them and finish cooking on the other side. Remove them from the oil with a slotted spoon and drain them on paper towels. Salt to taste. The straw potatoes are best if served immediately, but may be held in a warm oven for up to 20 minutes.

Using a carving knife, slice the beef into 1/2-inch-thick slices. Spoon the sauce onto warm dinner plates, arranging the morels decoratively around the perimeter. Place the straw potatoes at the left center and overlap the beef to the side. Garnish with a sprig of tarragon.

GRILLED LAMB CHOPS
WITH MUSTARD-ROSEMARY GLAZE

Serves 4

Our version of this classic combination is easy enough for a weeknight family dinner but, special enough for guests.

INGREDENTS

1/2 cup Dijon mustard

2 tablespoons soy sauce

1 large clove garlic, finely minced

1 teaspoon chopped fresh rosemary

Dash Tabasco sauce

1/4 teaspoon freshly ground black pepper

3 tablespoons olive oil

8 loin lamb chops

In a medium mixing bowl combine mustard, soy sauce, garlic, rosemary, Tabasco and black pepper. With a small whisk, incorporate the olive oil, drop by drop, until you have a smooth emulsified sauce with a consistency similar to mayonnaise. Generously coat both sides of the lamb chops with the mustard mixture and set aside, refrigerated, for at least 1/2 hour and up to 2 hours.

Over a medium-hot grill, cook the lamb for about 5 minutes on each side for medium rare. Remove from grill and brush with a little more of the mustard sauce if desired, or pass the remaining sauce separately for those who like a little extra zip. For a more pourable sauce, thin by whisking in a bit of warm chicken stock.

When accompanied by an assortment of seasonal grilled vegetables—eggplant, red onions, peppers of every hue, Roma tomatoes, summer squash of all shapes and colors—and garnished with abundant sprigs of fresh rosemary, this makes a gorgeous and festive presentation for a summer meal.

The mustard sauce is also wonderful for marinating chicken, pork and rabbit before grilling. In the winter, try it as a coating for roasted leg of lamb, whole chicken or pork loin and serve with roasted root vegetables, mashed potatoes and wilted seasonal greens.

INDEX

ACKNOWLEDGMENTS

Many talented people contributed to the realization of the
King Estate Pinot Noir Cookbook.
We would like to extend special thanks to:

Ed and Carolyn King for their enthusiastic and
ongoing commitment to the development of King Estate.

John Rizzo whose radiant photographs
give the book its extraordinary eye appeal.

Food stylist Carol Ladd for the painterly
composition of the food vignettes.

Funk & Associates Marketing Communications,
especially Beverly Soasey for her brilliant design and layout
and Marcia Schoelen for keeping us all on task.

Terry Ross for his editorial acumen.

Sulwyn Sparks and Julia Potter whose skill and
good humor in the kitchen were invaluable in
researching and testing all of the recipes.

Our master gardener, Jeanne Palzinski, who has
elevated the growing of fruits and vegetables to an art.

Winemakers Brad Biehl and Will Bucklin and their crew
for the exquisite wines that inspire our menus.

The entire King Estate staff for their advice and support.